DIRTY HANDS AND BUSTED KNUCKLES:

Copyright © 2021 by Dale Foster.

All rights reserved. No part of this book may be used or reproduced in any manner whatsoever without the express written permission of the publisher except for the use of brief quotations in a book review.

Printed in the United States of America

ISBN: 978-7358701-5-1 (paperback)

        978-7358701-6-8 (ebook)

First printing, 2021

JayMedia Publishing

Laurel, MD 20708

DIRTY HANDS AND BUSTED KNUCKLES:

A PRIMER FOR PRACTICAL LEADERSHIP

DALE FOSTER, DSL

Contents

LIST OF FIGURES 11
ACKNOWLEDGEMENTS 13
PREFACE 15
THE AUTHOR 21
COMPETENCY MAP 25
PROLOGUE: FOR WANT OF A NAIL 29
    LOGISTICS ENABLE OPERATIONS 29
    A NEW HUMAN ELEMENT PARADIGM 35
    FUTURE TRENDS. 36
SECTION I. PERSPECTIVE. 37
    SUMMARY 41
CHAPTER 1. KNOW THY SELF 43
    ASSESSMENTS. 44
    EMOTIONAL INTELLIGENCE 46
        Self-Awareness 47
        Self-Management 48
        Social Awareness 48
        Relationship Management 49
    THINKING DRIVES BEHAVIOR 49
    MENTORS 51
    MICROMANAGEMENT OR EMPLOYEE

EMPOWERMENT 52

CONFLICT 54

SUMMARY 56

CHAPTER 2. FUTURE ORIENTATION 57

THE TRANSITION BETWEEN PRESENT AND FUTURE 58

Future Orientation via Self-Reflection 59

Environmental scanning. 61

THE LEARNING ORGANIZATION. 63

THE S-CURVE PHENOMENON. 64

FUTURE SCENARIOS INSTEAD OF STATUS QUO. . . 65

SUMMARY 66

SECTION II. PEOPLE. 67

SUMMARY 70

CHAPTER 3. THE POWER OF LEADER ENGAGEMENT 71

EMOTIONAL INTELLIGENCE'S RELATIONSHIP MANAGEMENT. 73

UNDER THE MICROSCOPE 74

HUMILITY – IT IS HARD TO BE HUMBLE 75

COMMON COURTESY DRAWS A CROWD. 77

SUMMARY 78

CHAPTER 4. HIGH-QUALITY RELATIONSHIPS . . . 79

RELATIONSHIP MANAGEMENT 80

PERSONALITY ASSESSMENTS 81

PERFORMANCE MANAGEMENT. 82

THEORY BEHIND PRACTICE. 84

    Role Theory 84

    Social Exchange Theory 87

    Leader Member Exchange Theory 89

    Leadership is a System 89

  CULTURE DOMINATES: DIGNITY AND RESPECT . . . 91

  SUMMARY 95

CHAPTER 5. CHANGE PLUS SEVEN (C+7)™ 97

  CHARACTERISTICS OF CHANGE 98

  THE CARNAGE OF CHANGE 98

  THE ABCs OF RESISTANCE 100

    Affective 101

    Behavioral 102

    Cognitive 102

    BMC: Bitch, Moan, and Complain 103

  COMMUNICATION 104

  C+7™: SOCIALIZE THE CHANGE THEN IMPLEMENT 106

  SUMMARY 108

SECTION III. PROCESS 109

  SUMMARY 113

CHAPTER 6. PROCESS: THE PREREQUISITE TO EFFECTIVENESS 115

  THE PROCESS OF PROCESS: SIPOC 116

  THE SQUIGGLY LINE 119

  BLENDING PROCESS IMPROVEMENT APPROACHES 121

  CONTROLLED RELEASE OF WORK 124

  THE INTERSECTION OF CULTURE AND PROCESS . 126

WIP – WORK IN PROGRESS 127

SUMMARY 130

CHAPTER 7. VELOCITY 131

TOC PHILOSOPHY 132

ACCOUNTING IN A TOC ENVIRONMENT 133

THE TOC PROCESS 134

    Controlled Release of Work 136

    Slack 138

VELOCITY 139

    Lean/Lean Six Sigma 140

    Daily Math 142

    Agile 144

SUMMARY 145

CHAPTER 8. RAISING THE BAR 147

SEEING 148

    Conflict Cloud 149

    Value Stream Mapping (VSM) 151

    Gemba Walk 153

    Visual Management 154

    Metrics: The Critical Few 156

    Data Management and Dashboards 160

THE S-CURVE IMPROVEMENT APPROACH 161

EXECUTION TOOL: THE A3 163

AUTOPSY FAILURES 164

SUMMARY 165

SECTION IV: INTEGRATION 167

CHAPTER 9. BRAIDING THE ROPE 169

    CONFLUENCE 170

    RIPPLES 172

    POLITICS: THE ANTITHESIS OF COMMITMENT . . . 175

    ALIGNMENT 177

    SYSTEMS DYNAMICS 178

    SUMMARY 180

CHAPTER 10. BECOMING: THINGS TO PONDER . . 183

    LEADERSHIP ENGAGEMENT: KEY TO LEADERSHIP EFFECTIVENESS 184

    VISION CASTING 185

    COMMUNICATION 187

    CULTURE TRUMPS STRATEGY 188

    TRANSFORMATION 189

        The Butterfly 190

        The Leader 190

        The Organization 192

    COURAGE 194

    SUMMARY 196

BIBLIOGRAPHY 197

List of Figures

Figure 1: Content GPS & Waypoints. 25
Figure 2: Leader Engagement & Effectiveness 26
Figure 3: The Leadership Competency Triad 27
Figure 4: The Fishhook at Gettysburg. 30
Figure 5: Self-Reflection 39
Figure 6: Gallup Strengths. 45
Figure 7: Components of Emotional Intelligence 47
Figure 8: Citizens Against Virtually Everything 54
Figure 9: The Carnage of Change. 100
Figure 10: Resistance to Change 101
Figure 11: SIPOC – The Process of Process 110
Figure 12: The Squiggly Line 111
Figure 13: SIPOC – The Process of Process 118
Figure 14: The Squiggly Line 120
Figure 15: Statistical Process Control Chart 123
Figure 16: TOC Process Steps 133
Figure 17: TOC Conflict Cloud. 151
Figure 18: Gemba Walk 153
Figure 19: The S-Curve Technique 162
Figure 20: The Author's Farm A3 164
Figure 21: Confluence of People and Process 171
Figure 22: McKinsey 7-S Framework 173
Figure 23: Recovering the Disengaged Employees 177
Figure 24: The Stages of Organizational Behavior 178
Figure 25: McKinsey 7-S Framework 179
Figure 26: The Secret Language of Leadership. 188
Figure 27: Recovering the Disengaged Employees 194
Figure 28: Charge of the Light Brigade 195

Acknowledgements

Over the course of my career, I considered pursuing a doctoral degree several times. The timing never seemed right and the feedback I solicited from friends and colleagues with terminal degrees was consistently similar, i.e., that I was too old and that there would be no pay-off for the time invested. This changed when the Veteran's Affairs (VA) accepted my compensation claim and I encountered Ms. Gail Caldwell, a vocational rehabilitation specialist. She was blunt that my education was antiquated and was adamant that I start a third master's degree program. Over protests that such would do more harm than good, I started at Mercer University. I immediately began negotiating with Ms. Caldwell to shift into a terminal degree program. She went to bat for me and, after two semesters at Mercer University, placed me into the Doctor of Strategic Leadership program at Regent University. It was with her assistance and goodwill that I updated my antiquated education. I owe a special thanks to Gail for her support.

I also need to acknowledge a former commander in the Army National Guard, Major General Don Davis. Of all the commanders I served while in the Army system, he is the one who epitomized leadership. Savvy, well versed, and personable he set high standards and held soldiers accountable while creating an environment that was demanding, educational, and fun albeit stressful at times. Those who know General Davis know his personal tragedy and the manner by which he led. I pray I never need his inner strength. I am grateful for the lessons I learned under his command.

I have also had the pleasure to work in the consulting world with three individuals who mastered their fields and influenced me as an entrepreneur. Dr. Larry Newton, Dr. Satya Chakravorty (now deceased), and Mr. Ron Welch each exposed me to new learning and new ways to problem solve. I have used the lessons learned multiple times in different scenarios to help others enhance performance as they helped me.

The figures within are from the author's historical files to include work done with Mr. Ron Welch or from Google/Bing searches for appropriate free public domain clipart.

Finally, I acknowledge my bride of 38 years, Cindy, and my family – Ashley, Weston, Chase, and Kayla - for tolerating and encouraging me during this four-year period. I know I have been a burden and a pain on innumerable occasions. Blessed am I.

Preface

Leadership is ill-defined yet is an elemental component of organization effectiveness.[1] Regardless of level, every formal leader is a choreographer of resources, people, processes, and time as these variables interplay at the point where work is accomplished. If not properly choreographed then organization effectiveness is impeded. This choreography is a recurring phenomenon as every leader interaction either enhances or degrades daily performance. Concurrently, leadership also requires reflection[2] for not only current performance but also what comes next, i.e., the future which is the next hour, day, or week.[3]

The intent for this book is two-fold. First, I saw the need for an integrated approach to the academic literature that captured the essence of multiple topics normally contained in stand-alone books or articles, e.g., there are shelves filled with books on culture yet I have never been satisfied given the lack of "how to apply" this information in the real world. Other examples abound, e.g., the literature is replete with books and articles on process,

---

1 Peter G. Northouse, *Leadership: Theory and Practice* (Thousand Oaks, CA: Sage Publishing, 2016).
2 Daisy Shrimpton, Deborah McGann, Leigh M. Riby, "Daydream Believer: Rumination, Self-Reflection, and the Temporal Focus of Mind Wandering Content," *Europe's Journal of Psychology* 13, no. 4: 794-809, https://doi.org/10.5964/ejop.v13i4.1425.
3 James Canton, *Future smart: Managing the Game-Changing Trends that will Transform Your World* (Boston, MA: Da Capo Press, A Member of the Perseus Books Group, 2016).

but I have yet to encounter one that specifically alerted me to the essence of process from a leader's perspective. Second, I wanted to incorporate lessons that I have learned the hard way with the hope that readers will be able to avoid the mistakes I have made or experienced while in leadership. The title reflects the practicality of the approach in that theory and practice, if combined, lead to a proactive, hands-on approach to leadership or follower engagement. Of note, as Thomas Sowell indicated "There are no solutions. There are only tradeoffs."[4] This holds especially true in resource constrained environments which, typically, are found in most every organization.

The contents within are intended to represent key topics for aspirational or relatively new leaders as well as those in the throes of leadership engagement. The topics are based on first-hand experience gained over three decades dealing with the conundrums generated by what the author terms 'people in process'. The most detailed planning and most beautifully laid-out processes will fail given the human element if not intentionally and deliberately calibrated by the leader yet many in leadership never make this connection.[5] It is a critical connection that, when missed, generates unnecessary chaos and turmoil. One without the other is useless in the contemporary environment.[6]

---

4   Thomas Sowell, "Thomas Sowell>Quotes>Quotable Quotes," Goodreads.com, 2021, Quote by Thomas Sowell: "There are no solutions. There are only trade-offs." (goodreads.com).

5   Oxford Reference, "Helmuth von Moltke 1800-91 Prussian Military Commander," *Oxford Press, 2021*, Helmuth von Moltke —Oxford Reference.

6   Robert J. Anderson and W. A. Adams, *Mastering Leadership: An Integrated Framework for Breakthrough Performance and Extraordinary Business Results* (Hoboken, NJ: Wiley, 2016).

The major sections touch on the different aspects required for a holistic approach to operational success and expand the traditional roles and responsibilities view to include relationships; no effort will succeed if the power and pitfalls of relationship management are not understood and leveraged.[7] Until dark factories and work environments emerge — places run entirely by Artificial Intelligence and machines[8] — the relationship between leader and follower is vital to organizational success.[9] Leaders who do not leverage[10] this simple fact will experience more discord and failure than necessary.[11] Leaders must understand the feelings, behaviors, and thinking involved in work relationships and how to cultivate those relationships to gain not only discretionary effort but affective commitment to the organization.[12] High quality relationships are vital to success.[13] Developing,

---

7   Pascale M. LeBlanc and Vicente Gonzalez-Roma, "A Team Level Investigation of the Relationship between Leader-Member Exchange (LMX) Differentiation, and Commitment and Performance," *The Leadership Quarterly* 23, no. 3 (2012): 534-544, doi 10.1016/j.leaqua.201112.006.

8   Yan Vermeulen, "Lights Out: Manufacturing in the Dark", Odgers Berndtson, 2018, https://www.odgersberndtson.com/en-us/insights/manufacturing-in-the-dark.

9   Chester A. Schriesheim, Stephanie L. Castro, and Claudia C. Cogliser, "Leader-Member Exchange (LMX) Research: A Comprehensive Review of Theory, Measurement, and Data-Analytic Practices," *Leadership Quarterly* 10, no. 1 (1999): 63-113, https://doi.org/10.1016/s1048-9843(99)80009-5.

10 Donella H. Meadows, *Leverage Points: Places to Intervene in a System* (Hartland Four Corners, VT: Sustainability Institute, 1999).

11 Eddie Kilkelly, "Creating Leaders for Successful Change Management," *Strategic HR Review* 13, no. 3 (2014): 127-129, https://doi.org/10.1108/shr-01-2014-0004.

12 Eric H. Kessler, *Encyclopedia of Management Theory* (Los Angeles, CA: Sage Publications, 2003).

13 George B. Graen and Mary Uhl-Bien, "Relationship-Based Approach to Leadership: Development of Leader-Member Exchange (LMX) Theory of Leadership over 25 Years: Applying a Multi-Level Multi-Domain Perspective," *Leadership Quarterly* 6, no. 2 (1995): 219-247, https://doi.org/10.1016.1048-9843(95)90036-5.

cultivating, and sustaining these relationships is a fundamental leader skill.

One can just review the data on the incredible failure rate of change, over 75 percent,[14] to understand the author's viewpoint. This failure rate is accompanied by a decades' long history of over 70 percent of employees reporting their disengagement from the workplace.[15] The costs of this recurring failure in dollars, missed opportunity, and carnage[16] are likely incalculable. A quick Google search revealed that in 2008 approximately 100,000 MBAs were awarded each year in the US alone. That number increased to over 200,000 per year in 2014. There are millions of MBAs in the workplace, literally masters-of-business, yet these two statistics continue. Something is amiss. From the author's perspective the missing link is the artful blending of people with process to amplify organizational effectiveness.

Within this approach the author considers every leader a strategic operative in that every workstream and business unit within an organization should be considering how to improve performance 100-fold.[17] One sees this bold visioning in the likes of Elon Musk and Jeff Bezos as each works space-related initiatives designed to

---

14 Mark Collyer, "Communication – The Route to Successful Change Management: Lessons from the Guinness Integrated Business Programme," *Measuring Business Excellence* 5, no. 2 (2001). https://doi.org/10.1126/science.aau6026.

15 Jamie Lawrence, "What are the Causes & Nature of Employee Disengagement?" HRZone, 2016, https://www.hrzone.com/engage/employees/what-are-the-causes-nature-of-employee-disengagement.

16 Michael Stanleigh, "Effecting Successful Change Management Initiatives," *Industrial and Commercial Training* 40, no. 1 (2008): 34-37, https://doi.org/10.1108/00197850810841620.

17 Peter H. Diamandis and Steven Kotler, *Bold: How to Go Big, Create Wealth, and Impact the World* (Simon & Schuster, 2015).

transform humanity. It is this Big Hairy Audacious Goal (BHAG), Flying Pigs, or moonshot approach that generates innovation and transformation;[18] this approach also forces one to overcome the inertia of simply tweaking the status quo with changes around the edges.[19] Quite simply both type changes must be addressed and managed yet the BHAG, Flying Pig, or moonshot approach literally changes one's thinking.[20]

The dirty hands, busted knuckles approach to leadership requires this type of leadership thinking.[21] The contents below set the stage. It is up to you, the reader, to make the shift to a very active, very inspirational leadership style of engagement.[22] Beware: Soft skills required.[23]

---

18   John J. Sosik and Dongil Jung, *Full Range Leadership Development Pathways for People, Profit, and Planet* (New York, NY: Routledge, 2018).
19   Diamandis and Kotler, *Bold: How to Go Big.*
20   Diamandis and Kotler, *Bold: How to Go Big.*
21   Sosik and Jung, *Full Range Leadership.*
22   Sosik and Jung, *Full Range Leadership.*
23   Jeff Slattery, "Change Management," *Journal of Strategic Leadership* 4, no.2 (2013): 1-5, https://www.regent.edu/acad/global/publications/jsl/vol4iss2/jslvol4iss2.pdf#page=59.

The Author

Dale received his Doctor of Strategic Leadership (DSL) from Regent University in August 2021. He holds a Master of Strategic Studies from the U.S. Army War College and a Master of Public Administration from the former Georgia College. He is certified in both people and process centric techniques that are oriented toward amplifying organization effectiveness.

Dale retired from the Army Reserve after serving 33 years in the Army system, 30 as a commissioned officer. He served four command or CEO equivalent tours, three COO-equivalent tours which in Army vernacular were Assistant Chief of Staff for Operations assignments either as an S-3 or as a G-3, two tours in which he was the COO equivalent for logistics and maintenance operations, and two tours as the HR Director equivalent as an S-1. Dale deployed to Iraq from 2003-2004 during Operation Iraqi Freedom where he served as the 358 Civil Affairs Brigade G-3 and where he was integrated into the First Marine Expeditionary Force battle staff. Dale's terminal assignment was as a Faculty Instructor at the Army War College in the Department of Distance Education. Dale is a life-long practitioner and student of leadership.

Dale is also retired from Federal civil service. During his time in that system, he served in various leadership positions which culminated with his assignment as Deputy

Director for Business Operations in an Air Force manufacture, repair, and overhaul depot. Throughout his civil service career Dale was invariably responsible for change management via his ability to relate to people and his on-going studies of process improvement. Dale is certified as a Theory of Constraints Jonah and as a Lean Greenbelt. His on-going studies of process improvement solidified his recognition that process improvement efforts failed if leadership did not have positive relationships with the stakeholders, especially its employees.[24] This blending of a people orientation into process improvement resulted in Dale also becoming certified as a Myers Briggs practitioner and as both a Gallup Great Manager and a Gallup Strengths Performance Coach. Throughout this book you will see this theme of relationships undergirding all efforts to improve organization effectiveness. Dale's DSL studies further solidified his understanding that relationships make or break any change management effort.[25]

Throughout his career Dale struggled with the tendency to be focused on the future versus being in the present. This tendency caused tension and stress because his perspective was not always well received by those with a more present-oriented, firefighting perspective. It was not until he was exposed to the strengths management technique provided by the Clifton Strengths Finder assessment that he fully understood why he was often the outlier within the leadership team and in non-work

---

[24] Hock-Peng Sin, Jennifer D. Nahrgang, and Frederick P. Morgeson, "Understanding Why They Don't See Eye to Eye: An Examination of Leader-Member Exchange (LMX) Agreement," *Journal of Applied Psychology* 94, no. 4(2009): 1048-57, https://doi.org/10.1037/a0014827i.

[25] Sosik and Jung, *Full Range Leadership Development*.

areas as he sought to implement changes aligned to what he saw as new opportunities. The strengths awareness also helped clarify why he was so often placed in organizations that were not performing; turnarounds were his norm. Dale's top strength is Strategic[26] which tracks with his Perceiver orientation per the Romans 12 motivational gifts.[27] For better or for worse Dale has the ability to see through the fog well before others are aware issues or opportunities are forthcoming.[28] Many are taken aback by this trait even as many have benefitted.

Dale is currently a freelance business services consultant focused on Organization Effectiveness. He operates via Eagle3 Business Services, which is pending VA certification as a Service-Disabled Veteran Owned Small Business. He has supported multiple prime Federal contractors as a Subject Matter Expert in Change Management and Conflict Management. Supported agencies include the Air Force, the US Forest Service, the US Department of Agriculture, the Department of Homeland Security, and the IRS. He has also supported smaller private sector clients as well with Change Management efforts. Please contact him via LinkedIn: www.linkedin.com/in/dale-foster-008b1a146 or via email dale.foster.dsl@outlook.com.

---

26 Marcus Buckingham and Donald O. Clifton, Now , Discover Your Strengths: How to Develop Your Talents and Those of the People You Manage (London: Pocket Books, 2005).

27 Dorena DellaVecchio and Bruce E. Winston, "A Seven-Scale Instrument to measure the Romans 12 Motivational Gifts and a Proposition that the Romans 12 Gift Profiles might apply to Person-Job Fit Analysis," Published by the School of Leadership Studies, Regent University, 2004.

28 Daniel Trabucchi, Laurent Muzellec, and Sebastian Ronteau, "Sharing Economy: Seeing through the Fog," Internet Research 29, no. 5 (2019), https://doi.org/10.1108/INTR-03-2018-0113.

Competency Map

This section is intended to provide a high-level overview of the book's contents. In effect it serves as the book's GPS to alert the reader to the foundational competencies that the author considers especially important and that are thematic within the contents below. Each step in the map leads to a critical waypoint or milestone that serves as the reader's gauge to self-mastery of the material. Many readers will differ. Some will adamantly disagree. Critical thinking is perhaps underway when this occurs. If yes, that too is a leader competency. Goodness occurs.

Topic	Waypoint_1	Waypoint_2	End State
Perspective	Leader's worldview crystallizes after self-reflection.	Emotional Intelligence, humility, and civility are key.	How to relate to and with global diversity and differing worldviews.
People	Treat everyone as unique. Treat all with dignity and respect.	Social exchanges build trust. Trust is the superglue of relationships.	Affective commitment and discretionary effort result from high levels of trust.
Process	Effectiveness is greater than efficiency.	Throughput drives revenue.	Velocity of throughput requires efficiency at the constraint.
Integration	Dark factories are atypical.	People plus process gains effectiveness.	Leaders are competent in both people and process approaches.

Figure 1: Content GPS & Waypoints

A second approach to visualizing the contents is to use Figure 2 as a guide to see that leader engagement underpins every effort in the organization as people and/or process tend to be part of each business-related discussion. Figure 2 further depicts the confluence of people and process at the point where work is accomplished, or stated differently, where the organization's effectiveness is gained or lost. Figure 2 further amplifies the concept that leadership is a system with leadership engagement being the critical system component.

Figure 2: Leader Engagement & Effectiveness

Figure 3 addresses the three key leader competencies that the author believes underpins every single leader activity. The leader must possess a high degree of mental agility to survive, much less innovate, in the contemporary operating environment as new issues, problems, and opportunities manifest unexpectedly. The leader must also have a high degree of Emotional Intelligence to successfully and adroitly engage a highly diverse member and stakeholder population, a population that may have wildly divergent worldviews than the leader. And finally, the competency that leads to successful execution, the leader must be skilled and adroit in communications across seemingly ever-growing platforms.

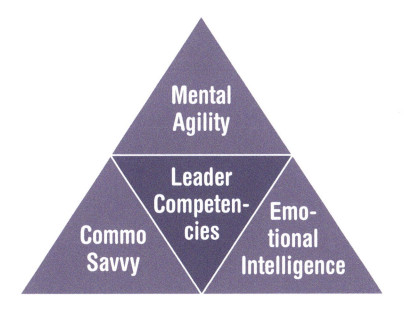

Figure 3: The Leader Competency Triad

The following chapters directly link to these differing macro perspectives. Each chapter provides more detail via differing lenses to provide the reader the opportunity to ponder how to deepen individual leader knowledge in the topical area while also providing the opportunity to begin real-time implementation of the key concepts under discussion. Leadership, albeit a system, is at the individual level also a thinking person's puzzle. One will see this thematically in the author's push for self-reflection as many times thinking provides the missing puzzle piece required for leadership effectiveness.

Prologue: For Want of a Nail

The Covid-19 pandemic has exposed more than political or "it's my body" concerns regarding the various vaccines. For organizations, the pandemic has shaken global supply chains to the core, and for many, has exposed the downside to the much heralded just-in-time (JIT) supply chains that provide consumers everything from washers and dryers to pick-up trucks. Amazingly, at the time of this writing effort, car dealerships near the author are mostly empty of new vehicles due to a chip shortage. The old proverb "For Want of a Nail" is most apropos as organizations and consumers suddenly realize how fragile the global supply system really is. It did not have to be this way. It could be time to reassess organic capacity and capability at both the organization and nation state levels.

LOGISTICS ENABLE OPERATIONS

Napoleon indicated "The amateurs discuss tactics: the professionals discuss logistics".[29] The importance of logistics cannot be overstated. Many study the Battle of Gettysburg for leadership vignettes and strategy; however, it is also germane to the contemporary student of

---

29   Napoleon Bonaparte, "The Amateurs Discuss Tactics: The Professionals Discuss Logistics," Quotefancy.com (n.d.), https://quotefancy.com/quote/870186/Napoleon-The-amateurs-discuss-tactics-the-professionals-discuss-logistics.

process and logistics if one understands time, distance, and the power of interior lines of communication. At Gettysburg one sees the interplay of these three variables in the combatants' formations on the battlefield, formations that ultimately looked like a giant fishhook.[30]

This fishhook provided the Union forces with interior lines of communications as compared to the Confederate forces exterior lines of communications. This concept of interior and exterior lines of communications speaks to the ease or difficulty of moving men and material during the ebb and flow of battle; yet it is easily adaptable to the contemporary global supply chain disruption underway as this book was in process. Time and distance are still relevant variables as is the concept of interior and exterior lines of communication.

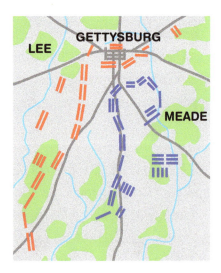

Figure 4: The Fishhook at Gettysburg

---

30 The fishhook map and discussion are from the author's notes from his time as a Faculty Instructor at the US Army War College. Gettysburg was frequently toured as part of leadership development during various staff rides.

Succinctly, Union forces were more agile with interior lines of communication due to proximity of men and material to the point of need, i.e., the fishhook geography allowed Union forces agility and relative ease of movement as compared to the Confederate forces who literally had miles of additional distance to cover to shift men and material before they could be applied at the point of need. Contemporary organizations with global supply chains are experiencing similar difficulties with time and distance given the geography involved in sustaining their logistical requirements. Simply stated, organizations with global supply chains are crashing because required items are simply not available at the point of need. The reasons for this are different from the Gettysburg analogy but the outcome is the same – contemporary organizations cannot sustain themselves using the current model.

Global supply chains increase time and distance of required logistics and are equivalent to exterior lines of communications. The underlying assumption of JIT-oriented supply chains requires environmental stability and is focused almost exclusively on cost reduction/cost avoidance regarding on-hand parts inventory. Efficiency is the goal with the understanding on-hand parts inventory is minimized to the maximum. Typically, there is no reserve or buffer of safety stock in case of system turbulence. The underlying assumption rules with the result many organizations, e.g., Ford and Tesla, are hamstrung due to the resultant bottlenecks that accrue due to the want of a small number of critical parts such as microchips. What were highly efficient supply chains are now hot messes as partially completed product is warehoused awaiting parts. The cost of this efficiency-first focus will be very high.

The earlier quote by Sowell, i.e., that there are no solutions only trade-offs,[31] is relevant as impacted organizations scramble to overcome earlier decisions related to process flow. At some point a trade-off was made to not maintain safety buffer inventory at the process constraint. This tracks with both Theory of Constraints and Lean approaches, respectively, cost management and waste elimination, while also speaking to the leader's need to understand both the art and science of logistics. Ultimately, the pendulum swung too far towards efficiency which is now reflected in said organizations being totally ineffective. Again, per Sowell, there are no easy solutions to this and the trade-off may well be a migration to a more hybrid approach, a new paradigm that better balances effectiveness and efficiency.

Technology may offer a bridge to the new hybrid approach wherein buffer or safety stocks of inventory are available on demand. As an example, the growing ability to leverage 3D and perhaps 4D printing may change the underlying assumption to one where it makes economic sense to have in-house manufacturing capacity and capability to mitigate, if not eliminate, the necessity of global supply chains. This would radically reduce the time and distance issues currently in play as a new approach to vertical integration is possible.

Without doubt, leaders responsible for supply chain management must reassess their current approach to obtain a better balance between effectiveness and

---
31 Sowell, "There are no Solutions."

efficiency. Risk management will be at the forefront of these process discussions and new decisions. Leaders would do well to recall Sun Tzu's Art of War admonitions regarding logistics: "Accordingly, if the army does not have baggage and heavy equipment, it will be lost; if it does not have provisions, it will be lost; if it does not have stores, it will be lost".[32] Sun Tzu spoke to logistics as one of the five factors for military success – if business is war, then logistics is paramount.[33]

Global supply chains in their current form negate Sun Tzu's forewarning.[34] This was glaringly exposed specifically within the various medical systems across the world as the ineffectiveness of nation-state planning for pandemic level events quickly became apparent. Within the United States (US), planning had been conducted at the highest levels; however, there was no execution of the plans as evidenced by long-depleted national inventory reserves of basic medical supplies. It was well known that stocks had been allowed to remain empty for years.[35]

The US population was also imperiled due to the lack of organic manufacturing capability of medical equipment and supplies. The JIT mentality that hamstrung the auto industry also hit the medical community hard as the US' almost total dependence upon China came to the

---

32   Ralph D. Sawyer, *Sun Tzu: Art of War* (Westview Press, 1994), 197.
33   Sawyer, *Sun Tzu: Art of War*, 167.
34   Sarah Fitzpatrick, "Why the Strategic National Stockpile isn't meant to solve a Crisis like Coronavirus," nbcnews.com, March 28, 2020, Why the Strategic National Stockpile isn't meant to solve a crisis like coronavirus (nbcnews.com).
35   Beth Reinhard and Emma Brown, "Face Masks and National Stockpile have not been substantially replenished since 2009," The Washington Post, March 10, 2020, Face masks in national stockpile of medical supplies have not been substantially replenished since 2009 - The Washington Post.

forefront as a single point of failure.[36] The most recognized item, the personal mask, is the easiest to identify yet the issue went much deeper as emergency powers had to be used to direct US industry to shift production to medical related items, e.g., respirators.[37] Over time the US shift was successful but the human cost was high – the loss of life was not the only adverse impact as trust in the system and in the leadership was also a casualty.

Many have subsequently recognized the unrelenting focus on efficiency was a key element in the world's inability to rapidly dampen the pandemic's harm; yet, the shift to a more balanced perspective via a 'lessons learned' approach will be difficult for most in leadership as cost of operations via the efficiency lens will be hard to overcome – it is likely too deeply ingrained in the MBA mindset. It will be the unique leader in the medical field or in academia to realize that the 2020 pandemic offers the opportunity for new business lines and approaches. Yet the opportunity does exist.

Interestingly, the US military offers the medical community and Congress an existing model for how things could be in the future. Per statute,[38] the US military maintains organic manufacturing capabilities at its various service depots even though the US military preference is to use defense contractors for such work. The

---

36 Fitzpatrick, "Strategic National Stockpile."

37 Jeffery Martin, "Trump Signs Emergency Bill to Make Companies Manufacture Medical Supplies to Fight Coronavirus," Newsweek, March 18, 2020, Trump Signs Emergency Bill to Make Companies Manufacture Medical Supplies to Fight Coronavirus (newsweek.com).

38 Congressional Research Service, "Defense Primer: Department of Defense Maintenance Depots," Congressional Research Service, November 7, 2017, Defense Primer: Department of Defense Maintenance Depots (fas.org).

redundancy is intentional to ensure the US maintains a military industrial base and industrial skills pipeline. But for this statutory requirement the US military would be totally dependent upon contractors. This model could be expanded to include organic manufacturing capability for medical items.

A NEW HUMAN ELEMENT PARADIGM

Once upon a time, before the big three consulting firms arguably changed the paradigm, large numbers of companies had long-term loyal middle managers and employees who could literally progress through the company from the mail room to the CEO position – in many cases the so-called company man. This was not necessarily a nirvana period of work relationships but people and companies were arguably in a much more symbiotic relationship than the current model. The big three consulting firms were able to shift this paradigm to one of reengineering oriented towards the company boards and executive staff, a paradigm focused almost exclusively on profits and dividends.

The result has been one of a shrinking middle class, gig workers, and social justice efforts to regain the so-called living wage. Part of this reengineering effort was a laser focus on efficiency with non-core functions divested or spun off into new organizations and the reengineered functionality contracted or outsourced, often to the same consultants who recommended the reengineering effort, given the functionality still was needed. The pandemic has shown the need to reconsider the employer-employee relationship to reassess the need for symbiotic loyalty and long-term commitment. A focus on not only employee fit but on long-term employee retention may be in order. A new human element paradigm is needed as we enter the new post-pandemic era.

FUTURE TRENDS

The author sees opportunity for both people and process paradigm shifts especially if organizational leaders understand the macro environment. The pandemic of 2020 and 2021 will not be the only shock to the system during the next decade as instability is almost guaranteed given the US' internal fracturing, the concurrent rise and assertion of global power by the Chinese, water related issues, the migration of thousands if not millions of people for various reasons, and the myriad of other wicked problems on the global continuum. The struggle between populists and globalists will become more strident as will the struggle between governance systems, i.e., capitalist or socialist orientations. Organizational leaders would do well to consider these environmental factors as part of their long-term strategic planning and vision casting especially as the social justice movement and the focus on hyper identity politics impact organizational cultures – leaders should expect more conflict as these variables interact and intersect with the more traditional effort to focus on the bottom line.

Organizations need to shift their foundations to rock versus sand to withstand these trends. Leadership with vision and foresight is much needed.

Section I. Perspective

"The more I learn, the less I know".[39]

"Knowing a great deal is not the same as being smart; intelligence is not information alone but also judgment, the manner in which information is collected and used".[40]

"Leadership is a complex puzzle that often goes unresolved".[41]

This book is intended to blend various theories related to organizational performance with proven, practical approaches that have resulted in success. In this section the author speaks to perspective or how one views the world as foundational to organizational success. This is an elemental aspect of leadership that is often overlooked given the author's experience simply because your perspective directly impacts your ability to establish the high-quality relationships required for a high performing organization.[42] This is the essence of leadership.

---

[39] An often used quote whose origin is not fully known but often attributed to Socrates.

[40] Carl Sagan, *"Knowing a Great Deal...,"* Goodreads.com, Accessed June 22, 2021, https://www.goodreads.com/quotes/897642-knowing-a-great-deal-is-not-the-same-as-being.

[41] Author unknown.

[42] Schriesheim et al., "LMX."

Leadership. A much-used word. Yet a word that has never been universally defined but is arguably recognized when it is seen or experienced.[43] Leadership is a nebulous concept for the daily practitioner given it is as much art as it is science.[44] It is this nebulous nature that causes consternation and, at times, carnage[45] when those in leadership positions fail to understand how to engage those who actually perform the organization's work.

It took several years before the author finally recognized that an essential part of engagement was understanding his worldview and that how he processed new information impacted how he interacted with others. At the time the author was not versed in Emotional Intelligence[46] *per se* but had the epiphany that his behavior and attitudes directly impacted others who, in turn, were responsible for the author's ultimate success. This epiphany led to the author seeking deeper understanding of this interaction. Part of his attempt to gain this deeper understanding was reflection.[47]

---

43 Northouse, *Leadership*.
44 Sawyer, *Sun Tzu: Art of War*.
45 Stanleigh, "Effecting Successful Change Management."
46 John Antonakis, Niel M. Ashkanasy, and Marie T. Dasborough, "Does Leadership need Emotional Intelligence?" *The Leadership Quarterly* 20, no. 2 (2009): 247-61, https://doi.org/10.1016/j.leagua.2009.01.006.
47 Shrimpton et al., "Daydream Believer."

Figure 5: Self Reflection

Reflection[48] is a powerful self-development tool that should be scheduled along with work requirements, exercise, and vacation. The time spent should include better understanding one's personal worldview[49] simply because this knowledge becomes a baseline for understanding how others, with different worldview perspectives,[50] will both react and relate to your leadership. It does not take much effort to see this in the real-world as politics, climate, and green energy serve as examples of polarization that spills over into the workplace. These are complex, emotional topics that are only further exacerbated in the

---

48   Zhining Wang, Shaohan Cai, Mengli Liu, Dandan Liu, and Lijun Meng, "The Effects of Self-Reflection on Individual Intellectual Capita," *Journal of Intellectual Capital*, (2020): 1469-1930, https://doi.org/10/1108/jic-03-2019-0043.

49   Simon Maria Kopf, "A Problem for Dialogue: Can World-Views be Rational?" New Blackfriars, 2017: 284-98, https://doi.org/10.1111/nbfr.12328.

50   Eileen Crist, "Reimagining the Human: A Human-Centric Worldview is Blinding Humanity to the Consequences of Our Actions," *Science* 362, no. 6420 (2018): 1242-44, https://doi.org/10.1126/science.aau6026

workplace by the global nature of the workforce with all the cultural implications that leaders must inevitably navigate with every single interaction.[51] For both current and prospective leaders having conscious awareness of one's worldview, in essence one's beliefs and values, sets the stage for success in cultivating, developing, and sustaining the high-quality relationships that amplify organization effectiveness.[52]

The vital point to be emphasized is simple: Your worldview underlies each and every interaction because it is the filter through which you interpret and evaluate life experiences.[53] Each and every interaction with an organizational member is influenced by this hence the need for explicit awareness. Ultimately, every interaction is a negotiation wherein the leader is trying to gain member acceptance and support at the end of the day; there may not be a conscious awareness but influence and persuasion are constantly in play even if the effort is not recognized as such.[54]

The two chapters that follow are intended to shape the reader's thinking relative to perspective. Each is oriented to posturing the reader to lead change in a most turbulent environment.

---

51 Marjaana Gunkel, Christopher Schlägel, and Robert L. Engle, "Culture's Influence on Emotional Intelligence: An Empirical Study of Nine Countries," *Journal of International Management* 20, no. 2 (2014): 256-74, https://doi.org/10.1016/j.intman.2013.10.002.

52 LeBlanc and Gonzalez-Roma, "LMX."

53 David Kim, Dan Fisher, and David McCalman, "Modernism, Christianity, and Business Ethics: A Worldview Perspective," *Journal of Business Ethics* 90, no. 1 (2009): 115-121, https://doi.org/10.1007/s10551-009-0031-2.

54 Robert B. Cialdini, *Influence: Science and Practice* (Boston, MA: Allyn & Bacon, 2009).

SUMMARY
- Leadership is both art and science.
- One's personal worldview filters life experiences.
- Self-reflection is a powerful tool to gain insight into one's worldview.

Chapter 1. Know Thy Self

"He who knows others is wise; he who knows himself is enlightened".[55]

This could be a very complex chapter given the title but that is not the intent. The intent is knowing yourself so that you can maximize organizational performance at any level of the organization by positively leveraging the relationships that directly and indirectly affect your area of responsibility. In this case leveraging is understanding how the people with whom you work relate to your leadership, or not, and how those relationships drive high performance, or not. Leadership is not universally defined[56] but it always includes choreographing resources, processes, people, and time. The research is clear – change efforts fail due to the human element.[57] Leadership is responsible for relationship management. The following sections address critical aspects of knowing yourself which, in turn, impact your ability to positively leverage or amplify the power of high-quality relationships in the organization.[58]

---

55 Lao Tzu, "He who knows others is wise; he who knows himself is enlightened," Goodreads.com, Accessed 2021, Know Thyself Quotes (249 quotes) (goodreads.com).
56 Northouse, *Leadership*.
57 Collyer, "Communication."
58 LeBlanc and Gonzalez-Roma, "LMX."

ASSESSMENTS

There are multiple assessments that can assist you in better understanding how you perceive and react to issues.[59] These can be very powerful if coupled with deliberate intent to understand the implications relative to positively leveraging work relationships.[60] Introverted leaders still must engage and interact even though such is not the preferred style. Leaders who do not have the strategic strength in their Top 5 or 10 must still work within the strategic domain. Knowing these type characteristics can help you as you engage and interact. At a high level this awareness is part of being emotionally intelligent as you master the self-awareness competency within the EI framework.[61] Being self-aware in a non-egotistical manner will better posture you to positively interact with those who invariably will have different worldviews, opinions, and goals than you.[62]

---

59 Sosik and Jung, *Full Range Leadership Development*.
60 LeBlanc and Gonzalez-Roma, "LMX."
61 Pearl R. Smith, "Enhancing Your Emotional Intelligence: Manage Emotions to get Results You Want!" 2013, PowerPoint presentation to Mercer University MSOL students, McDonough, GA in 2017.
62 Kopf, "A Problem for Dialogue."

Strategic Thinking	Relationship Building
• Analytical • Context • Futuristic • Ideation • Input • Intellection • Learner • Strategic	• Adaptability • Connectedness • Developer • Empathy • Harmony • Includer • Individualization • Positivity • Relator
Influencing	**Executing**
• Activator • Command • Communication • Competition • Maximizer • Self-Assurance • Significance • Woo	• Achiever • Arranger • Belief • Consistency • Deliberative • Discipline • Focus • Responsibility • Restorative

Figure 6: Gallup Strengths

Below is a partial list of assessments that can help you gain insight into the uniqueness of you, the individual leader. Each provides a different perspective whereas together the reader will gain a more holistic understanding. Do not analyze the options…go with your first instinct to obtain the most accurate outcome. This understanding is the first step to gaining a high degree of Emotional Intelligence, the key to attaining the attributes and characteristics of the Transformational or Servant Leader.[63]

1. StrengthsFinder 2.0 | EN - Gallup (Secular)
2. VIA Character Strengths Survey & Character Reports | VIA Institute (Secular)
3. https://www.gifttest.org/ (Christian)
4. Definition of Spiritual Gifts | Gifts Test (Christian)

---

[63] Crystal J. Davis, *Servant Leadership and Followership: Examining the Impact on Workplace Behavior* (Cham, Switzerland: Palgrave McMillan, 2017).

EMOTIONAL INTELLIGENCE

Emotional Intelligence reflects your capacity to understand and recognize how emotions and feelings interplay within individuals and within relationships between and among individuals and groups.[64] This recognition becomes a technique through which leaders can positively leverage the intersection of emotions and feelings with performance while dampening the likelihood of conflict within the organization.[65] The author was skeptical of this topic when he first encountered the term; however, he has grown to better understand EI's importance relative to organizational effectiveness. No matter the level of person with whom you interact the components of EI are in play[66] and you are either influencing or being influenced as a result.[67] If not understood, the negative dynamics of EI can ripple through an organization and serve as the root cause of conflict, resistance to change, and general malaise.[68] The components of EI can be considered components of a strategic management competency - a competency that overlays multiple relationship theories that will be discussed in further detail in subsequent chapters. For purposes of this section an introduction to EI and its components will set the stage for better understanding as you continue reading.[69]

---

[64] Smith, "Enhancing your Emotional Intelligence."
[65] Ibid.
[66] Antonakis et al., "Does Leadership Need Emotional Intelligence?"
[67] Cialdini, *Influence*.
[68] Gary Oster, "Listening to Luddites: Innovation Antibodies and Corporate Success," Regent Blackboard, (n.d.).
[69] Antonakis, "Does Leadership Need Emotional Intelligence?"

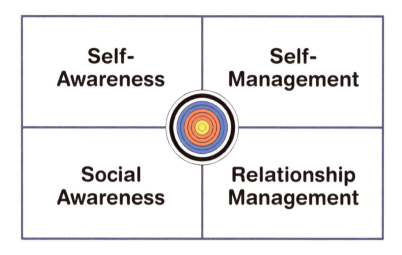

Figure 7: Emotional Intelligence

Self-Awareness

This is the key EI component for this chapter as it relates directly to recognition and acceptance, that as a leader, your emotions and feelings impact not only you but all those with whom you interact. Key considerations include being attuned to your emotional triggers and the resulting feelings and behaviors; whether or not you can laugh at yourself; whether or not you are graceful and receptive when receiving feedback and criticism; and whether or not you are self-confident and self-assured. If you are easily irritated, are brusque and abrasive with others, and are not open to feedback, you do not have a deep sense of self-awareness. Many in leadership scoff at the idea of self-reflection but this technique is a pre-requisite for gaining deeper self-awareness.[70] Research in leader development, regardless of domain, speaks to the power

---
70   Wang et al., "The Effects of Self-Reflection."

of journaling as a means to better understand oneself, e.g., Benjamin Franklin journaled daily as he attempted to improve his character and overall effectiveness.[71]

Self-Management

Self-Management speaks directly to the appropriate control of your emotions and feelings. Your reputation in the organization precedes you in this area, e.g., if you are known to be brusque and short-tempered or that you do not handle stress well most everyone in the organization already knows this. Conversely, if you are relatable and approachable these characteristics are also widely known. Signs of struggle in this area include impulsive behaviors, difficulty surmounting challenges, and undue stress in a changing environment. Signs of strength include controlled and restrained behavior under stress, calculated risk taking, and seeing opportunities where others see threats.[72]

Social Awareness

This domain speaks to the ability to recognize emotions and feelings in others.[73] Social awareness and empathy are almost interchangeable in this regard as unspoken communications or being attuned to body language may

---

[71] Donald J. Robertson, "The Stoicism of Benjamin Franklin," Medium, February 5, 2020, https://medium.com/stoicism-philosophy-as-a-way-of-life/the-stoicism-of-benjamin-franklin-21ed64abb4ab.

[72] Shagini Udayar, Marina Fioria, and Elise Bausseron, "Emotional Intelligence and Performance in a Stressful Task: The mediating Role of Self-Efficacy," *Personality and Individual Differences* 156 (April 2020): 109790.

[73] Smith, "Enhancing Your Emotional Intelligence."

be the key to understanding this area.[74] A key sign of struggle in this area is that you do not actively listen; you are planning your response instead.[75] A secondary sign of struggle in social awareness is that you either do not care how others feel or you assume you know. Active listening and relating to others, even when you disagree, are signs of social awareness strength.[76]

Relationship Management

This is the secondary focus area for this chapter as relationship management is vital to enhancing organizational effectiveness.[77] This will be specifically addressed in a later chapter; however, for this introduction it is imperative to know that relationship management is truly how you, the leader, manage other people's emotions.[78] It is within this domain that visioning, inspiration, aspiration, conflict management, change management, and teaming all occur – those intangible leadership issues that require followership else the organization fails.[79]

THINKING DRIVES BEHAVIOR

The ancient Greek and Roman practitioners of Stoicism believed in meditation and self-reflection as means to

---

74 Amy Cuddy, "Your Body Language Shapes Who You Are | Amy Cuddy," YouTube, 2012, https://www.ted.com/talks/amy_cuddy_your_body_language_shapes_who_you_are.
75 Smith, "Enhancing Your Emotional Intelligence."
76 Ibid.
77 Sin et al., "Understanding Why They Don't See Eye to Eye."
78 Udayar et al., "Emotional Intelligence and Performance."
79 Petra Düren, "Change Communication Can Be So Simple! The Empathic Change Communication Style," *Library Management* 37, no. 89 (2016): 398-409, https://doi.org/10.1108/lm-01-2016-0006.

improve character.[80] These ancients typically examined their daily efforts by asking three questions at the end of the day:

1. What have I done wrong?
2. What have I done well?
3. What have I omitted that I ought to have done?

Benjamin Franklin adopted this philosophical approach to improve his character and recorded his self-assessments in a stylized journal.[81] Even though intended to improve moral character the approach indicates that routine self-examination, i.e., thinking through one's actions, can improve performance due to behavioral changes.[82] The key is understanding that how you think impacts your behavior.[83] Succinctly, thinking is the foundation for all behavior as thinking drives our response to every situation.[84] This is an important part of relationship management because of the routine exposure to different ideas and opposing opinions that invariably surface in the global workplace.[85] From a big picture perspective understanding the thinking-drives-behavior connection almost mandates civility is your behavioral norm to dampen the high probability of conflict in the

---

[80] Robertson, "The Stoicism of Benjamin Franklin."
[81] Robertson, "The Stoicism of Benjamin Franklin."
[82] Shrimpton et al., "Daydream Believer."
[83] Robertson, "The Stoicism of Benjamin Franklin."
[84] Teal McAteer, "Top 3 Tips for Understanding How Thinking Affects Behaviour," Degroote School of Business, 2016, https://www.degroote.mcmaster.ca/articles/top-3-tips-understanding-thinking-affects-behaviour/.
[85] Paula Caligiuri, *Cultural Agility: Building a Pipeline of Successful Global Professionals* (San Francisco, CA: Jossey-Bass, 2011).

workplace – and the research indicates civility is highly related to EI's self-awareness component.[86]

MENTORS

Leaders at all levels need mentors who are willing and available to provide the often-needed reality check and to help the leader continue both personal and professional development.[87] Many shy away from this due to the perception of being political; however, politics and power are inherent parts of every organization.[88] The counterbalance to political concerns is to ensure all mentoring efforts are ethically correct.[89] It is a critical part of self-awareness[90] to recognize and accept that you will not succeed without continued development and, conversely, that you play a critical role in developing your employees and team members as a means to gain both affective commitment and trust.[91] In accordance with role theory these engagements are the stepping stones for the high-quality relationships that define high performance organizations.[92]

---

86 Christine Lynne Porath, *Mastering Civility: A Manifesto for the Workplace* (New York, NY: Grand Central Publishing, 2016).
87 Kilkelly, "Creating Leaders for Successful Change Management."
88 Glenys M. Drew, "Enabling or "Real" Power and Influence in Leadership," *Journal of Leadership Studies* 4, no. 1 (2010): 47-58, https://doi.org/10.1002/jls.20154.
89 Joanne B. Ciulla, Ethics, *The Heart of Leadership* (Santa Barbara, CA: Praeger, 2014).
90 Smith, "Enhancing Your Emotional Intelligence."
91 Kilkelly, "Creating Leaders for Successful Change Management."
92 LeBlanc and Gonzales-Roma, "LMX."

MICROMANAGEMENT OR EMPLOYEE EMPOWERMENT

The issue in this section is understanding and awareness of how your leadership style impacts organizational effectiveness. There are times when the spirit crushing micromanagement style is required; however, this approach should be rarely and judiciously used due to its debilitating impact on trust which is directly linked to high performance.[93] In a subsequent section process will be addressed. Just be cognizant that process approaches that call for agility and efficiency typically call for direct employee empowerment to identify and execute improvement opportunities. Leaders who must be in total control will adversely impact not only the improvement effort but also customer relations.[94]

Micromanagement is anathema to organizational effectiveness. Your goal should be to ensure your employees or team members are not only upskilled but coached on expectations and how their performance links to organizational effectiveness as opposed to micromanaging task performance. The academic research behind the above statements is very clear that leaders and members evolve through multiple steps before high-quality relationships are established.[95] In the first two steps the employee or

---

[93] Paula Matos Marques Simoes, Fundacao Dom Cabral, Belo Horizonte, and Mark Esposito, "Improving Change Management: How Communication Nature Influences Resistance to Change," *Journal of Management Development* 33, no. 4 (2014): 324–41, https://doi.org/10.1108/jmd-05-2012-0058

[94] Michael L. George, David Rowlands, Marc Price, and John Maxey, *The Lean Six Sigma Pocket Toolbook: A Quick Reference Guide to Nearly 100 Tools for Improving Process Quality, Speed, and Complexity* (New York: Toronto: McGraw-Hill, 2005).

[95] Sin et al., "Understanding Why They Don't See Eye to Eye."

team member is not only accepting work assignments but gauging you as a leader, i.e., are you providing clear expectations, assisting with learning curve elimination, and providing the appropriate resources required for success. If you are, the employee or team member becomes more receptive to assuming more expansive assignments and, with more positive interaction, will provide effort well beyond contractual or position description expectations.[96] These engagement interactions are where trust is gained or lost.[97] Micromanagement kills trust.

A quote from General Patton speaks to this directly: "Don't tell people how to do things, tell them what to do and let them surprise you with their results".[98] This is difficult for many in leadership hence the need for self-reflection and self-awareness[99] as you consider how you affect others and how that effect impacts the organization. Most do not have the self-confidence of General Patton.

With this self-awareness of trust at the forefront of your thinking be aware that you will never eliminate conflict in the workplace. No matter how diligent you are in cultivating high-quality relationships you will not be able to reach everyone; without fail there will be some employees who do not reach the point of high-quality relationships[100] or with whom you cannot establish such

---

[96] Kessler, *Encyclopedia of Management Theory*.

[97] Alan Lawler, "LMS Transitioning to Moodle: A Surprising Case of Successful, Emergent Change Management," *Australasian Journal of Educational Technology* 27, no. 7 (2011): 1111-1123, https://doi.org/10.14742/ajet.907.

[98] George S. Patton, "Don't Tell People How to do Things, Tell Them What to do and Let Them Surprise You with the Results," BrainyQuote.com, (n.d.), https://www.brainyquote.com/quotes/george_s_patton_159766.

[99] Wang et al., "Self-Reflection and Employee Creativity."

[100] Northouse, *Leadership*.

relationships.[101] How you manage conflict is also part of knowing yourself. The section below will discuss conflict considerations.

Figure 8: Citizens Against Virtually Everything – CAVE People

CONFLICT

Conflict avoidance tends to be the preferred technique for many in leadership.[102] One sees this during performance counseling and reviews in many situations as the leader is uncomfortable addressing legitimate performance concerns. The problem with this approach is obvious but often not considered, i.e., that everyone else in the

---

101 Jacqueline A. Gilbert, Deana M. Raffo, and Toto Sutarso, "Gender, Conflict, and Workplace Bullying: Is Civility Policy the Silver Bullet?" *Journal of Managerial Issues* 25, no. 1: 79-98, http://www.jstor.org/stable/43488159.

102 Neil H. Katz and Linda T. Flynn, "Understanding Conflict Management Systems and Strategies in the Workplace: A Pilot Study," *Conflict Resolution Quarterly* 30, no. 4(2013): 393-410, https://doi.org/10.1002/crq.21070.

organization is acutely aware that the issue is festering. Failure to address an issue is a leadership failure.

A second issue for the leader is that, after avoidance, another default conflict technique is to seek compromise.[103] This approach may lead to short-term issue resolution; however, those involved in the compromise invariably perceive a loss occurred which becomes a source of future irritation between the parties. Comprise may be required but the future impact and associated costs must be considered.

The question becomes is the leader unskilled in conflict management techniques that are universal, repeatable, and measurable. These skills are outside the scope of this chapter but are available and can be used in every conflict situation. This allows a consistent approach to conflict management while providing an individualized approach to resolution. This section is not intended to address conflict management as a theme but to ensure you, as a leader, understand that you must be skilled in conflict management and that you must ensure that conflict resolutions, to the extent practicable, align to the organization's vision and goals.

Until true dark factories emerge in which the human element is totally displaced[104] you must know how you react to and manage conflict; you will contend with the phenomenon routinely as you engage with superiors,

---

103 Katz and Flynn, "Understanding Conflict Management Systems."
104 Vermeulen, "Lights Out."

peers, subordinates, and stakeholders.[105] The dark factory concept[106] infers the future, a consideration many in leadership allow to happen versus shaping it.[107]

SUMMARY

- Self-awareness is a paramount requirement for leaders.
- Mentoring is a powerful technique to improve as a leader.
- Your personal style affects high-quality relationships which are key to attaining high organizational performance.
- Conflict can be dampened but not eliminated – ensure you are skilled in conflict management techniques that are universal but provide for individualized resolutions.
- Never stop your personal and professional development.

---

105 Christina Parker, "Practicing Conflict Resolution and Cultural Responsiveness within Interdisciplinary Contexts: A Study of Community Service Practitioners," *Conflict Resolution Quarterly* 32, no. 3 (2015): 325-357, https://doi.org/10.1002/crq.21115.

106 Vermeulen," Lights Out."

107 James Greybey, "NatGeo's 'Year Million' is an Educational 'Black Mirror'," Inverse, 2017, Accessed June 22, 2021, https://www.inverse.com/article/31604-year-million-national-geographic-documentary-black-mirror-ai-future.

Chapter 2. Future Orientation

"Whatever you can do, or dream you can do, begin it. Boldness has genius, power, and magic in it. Begin it now".[108]

"The secret of your future is hidden in your daily routine".[109]

What you dream can be. To convert dreams into reality requires action. With a few keystrokes you can suddenly be inundated with Google results that speak to the future yet many seemingly discount the deeper essence of a future orientation. The author has encountered a long list of people in mid to senior leadership positions who indicated they are so focused on fighting today's fires that they have no time to think about, much less reflect upon, next week's, or next quarter's work. A ten-year vision or plan? Get real.

Then the pandemic hits and the future has compressed upon them as a distributed workforce and concerns about employee well-being as a productivity multiplier become

---

[108] Scott Berkun, T*he Myths of Innovation* (Sebastopol, CA: O'Reilly Media, 2007).

[109] Mike Murdock, "The secret of your future is hidden in your daily routine," BrainyQuote.com, 2021, Future Quotes - BrainyQuote.

the norm.[110] Anecdotal conversations indicate cognitive dissonance abounds in both leadership and member ranks as people, in many instances, have been forced to adapt to disruptive change.[111] As a leader, understanding the future should be a core competency instead of a reactive measure when the future crashes down upon you. The following sections are intended to introduce you to key components of gaining a future orientation.

THE TRANSITION BETWEEN PRESENT AND FUTURE

The subtitle is simple yet the concept within is psychologically complex. Technically, the future includes the next nano second but realistically understanding the transition point is ambiguous at best as there are arguably overlap and fuzziness involved. This fuzziness impacts your decision making unless you develop a conscious future orientation.[112] Psychologically, you have a present self and a future self within your brain and these two entities struggle as to the transition.[113] The shift to a future orientation must initially occur internally before you can adapt your approach to the organization: Being in the present is a magical time, much easier than expending

---

110 Erica Volini, Craig Eaton, Jeff Schwartz, David Mallon, Yves Van Durme, Maren Hauptmann, Rob Scott, and Shannon Poynton, "Diving Deeper: Five Workforce Trends to Watch in 2021," Deloitte Insights, 2020, Exploring workforce trends 2020 | Deloitte insights.

111 Simoes et al., "Improving Change Management."

112 Daniel Goldstein, "The Battle between Your Present and Future Self," YouTube, 2011, https://www.youtube.com/watch?v=t1Z_oufuQg4.

113 Goldstein, " The Battle between Your Present and Future Self."

energy and thought imagining future opportunities and requirements.[114]

As a leader you must understand that neither the person you are today nor the organization that you lead will remain the same as they are today in the future...changes will occur haphazardly or intentionally depending upon your actions.[115] If a future orientation is not a natural strength for you then you should work to develop it else accept that stagnation and missed opportunities will be your norm. Self-reflection, an internal technique, and environmental scanning, an external technique, are two tools that can assist you in better understanding the future.

Future Orientation via Self-Reflection

Every human being experiences what is called mind-wandering by psychologists, a phenomenon that can occupy up to fifty percent of our awake time, and that takes us away from whatever we are doing in the present moment.[116] This mind-wandering, or distraction, is typically uncontrolled unless the person adopts a very high degree of self-control and yet it has very positive outcomes as people can literally time travel and conduct future planning while in this state of distraction.[117] The research into mind-wandering indicates it is frequently prospectively or future-focused and increases the person's sense of positivity.[118] This positive focus is also

---

114 Dan Gilbert, "The Psychology of Your Future Self," YouTube, 2014, https://www.youtube.com/watch?v=XNbaR54pj4.
115 Canton, *Future Smart*.
116 Shrimpton et al., "Daydream Believer."
117 Ibid.
118 Ibid.

referred to as self-reflection which involves curiosity, increased creativity, and goal-setting.[119]

Self-reflection is actually an intellectual event that provides the practitioner a means of not only of goal-setting, but a medium in which the person can think from differing perspectives and engage in analogous comparisons of ideas.[120] For the leader it is important to understand that self-reflection provides the opportunity to both evaluate and clarify one's thoughts, feelings, and behaviors relative to effectiveness.[121] If one adopts self-reflection as an on-going technique the outcome, like any exercise, is increased creativity and mental flexibility, or stated more directly, increased mental cognition, abilities, and performance.[122]

Self-reflection has powerful implications for leaders as it provides the means and the opportunity to literally inspect one's thoughts, feelings, and behaviors which has multiple applications within the leadership domain,[123] e.g., how leaders need to be emotionally intelligent.[124] Self-reflection is also a technique of choice for making a future orientation part of your leadership competencies. Scheduling time for deliberate future-oriented self-reflection institutionalizes the approach, and like any other exercise, embeds the process into your muscle memory.

How you conduct self-reflection is a personal choice; however, a proven approach is to journal to codify the

---

119 Ibid.
120 Wang et al., "The Effects of Self-Reflection."
121 Ibid.
122 Ibid.
123 Ibid.
124 Udayar et al., "Emotional Intelligence and Performance."

exercise in writing.[125] The act of writing triggers the brain in such a way that it does not differentiate between the physical act of writing and the imagining that is on-going; both merge as reality within the brain and generates positivity similar to the runner's high.[126] Journaling about the future allows you to see and think differently about the future which becomes a very powerful antecedent for leading change.[127]

Environmental scanning

Environmental scanning is an external technique designed to depict organizational opportunities and threats via the systematic review of an organization's internal and external environment.[128] In the contemporary environment, technological trends tend to be a major source of both opportunity and threat due to the rapid adoption of Artificial Intelligence, Big Data, and the use of machine learning to transform society at large.[129] The contemporary leader, regardless of level, needs to be aware of these trends to anticipate the immediacy of impact as well as how to leverage these trends to enhance performance.[130] If adopted, environmental scanning can help you avoid losing competitive advantage as you assimilate, anticipate, and plan for different scenarios that may arise

---

125 Nicole Lepera, "How to Future-Self-Journal," YouTube, 2019, How to Future-Self Journal - YouTube .

126 Lepera, "How to Future-Self-Journal."

127 Ibid.

128 Hitesh Bhasin, "Importance of Environmental Scanning," Marketing91, 2019, https://www.marketing91.com/environmental-scanning.

129 Peter H. Diamandis and Steven Kotler, *The Future is Faster than You Think: How Converging Technologies Are Transforming Business, Industries, and Our Lives* (New York, NY: Simon and Schuster Paperbacks, 2020).

130 Canton, *Future Smart*.

as threats and to position yourself to leverage opportunities faster than your competition.[131]

Environmental scanning enhances your relevance within the environment due to the data collection and analysis that occurs; new approaches and new strategies likely will be discussed and implemented that allow you to stay abreast of market changes.[132] The end result is that you develop a new future-oriented mental model that opens your receptiveness to new ideas, new possibilities, and most critically, innovation opportunities.[133] A key take-away reminder is that for most individuals the future will seamlessly blend with the present and simply occur[134] with no consideration that it, the future, could have been anticipated and shaped into multiple possible futures.[135]

At a minimum, the classical SWOT analysis tool[136] and the more positively oriented SOAR analysis tool[137] are available to help you analyze the data collected during self-reflection and environmental scanning: Respectively these are Strengths, Weaknesses, Opportunities, & Threats and Strengths, Opportunities, Aspirations, &

---

131 Thomas J. Chermack, *Scenario Planning in Organizations: How to Create, Use, and Assess Scenarios* (San Francisco, CA: Berrett-Koehler, 2011).
132 Bhasin, "Importance of Environmental Scanning."
133 Diamandis and Kotler, The Future is Faster Than You Think.
134 Gilbert, "The Psychology of Your Future Self."
135 Chermack, *Scenario Planning*.
136 Bhasin, "Importance of Environmental Scanning."
137 Jacqueline Stavros, David Cooperrider, and D. Lynn Kelley, "Strategic Inquiry with Appreciative Intent: Inspiration to SOAR!" *AI Practitioner: International Journal of Appreciative Inquiry*, (2003).

Results.[138] A third tool, the A3,[139] takes the SWOT and SOAR analysis to an actionable strategic plan as discrete actions are required to implement a desired future state. Power and leverage are gained if all three are used to gain differing perspectives of what could be for the organization.[140]

THE LEARNING ORGANIZATION

This topic is a book unto itself as Senge so famously demonstrated.[141] The concept is included in this chapter because it powerfully demonstrates the future orientation every leader, regardless of level, should consciously develop and apply given the dynamics and turbulence of the contemporary operating environment.[142] Learning should be considered a key component of any future orientation to obviate stagnation and loss of relevance in the market; competitive edge can be lost if allowed to dull – deliberate learning is the iron that sharpens iron[143] in a highly competitive, ever changing environment. As an example, contemporary leaders should be thinking through the impact of the so-called fourth industrial revolution on the organization as Artificial Intelligence

---

138 Stavros et al., "Strategic Inquiry."
139 Durward K. Sobek and Art Smalley, *"Understanding A3 Thinking: A Critical Component of Toyota's PDCA Management System* (Boca Raton: CRC Press, 2008).
140 Gareth Morgan, *Images of Organizations*, (Thousand Oaks, CA: Sage Publications, Inc., 2006).
141 Peter M. Senge, *The Fifth Discipline Fieldbook* (London: N. Brealey, 1994).
142 Chermack, *Scenario Planning.*
143 *New American Standard Bible* (Lockman Foundation,1995), https://bible.knowing-jesus.com.

and robotics proliferate.[144] More specifically, the dark factory[145] must be understood relative to resourcing the technology, interfacing the remnant human element, upskilling or retraining the remnant human element to operate within this dark environment, identifying consumers, and a myriad of other topics to ensure viability and success before Artificial Intelligence in all its forms overwhelms current organization design. Learning is inherent in these considerations and is a prerequisite to the transformative impacts headed our way.

THE S-CURVE PHENOMENON

The S-Curve arguably is both a philosophy and a technique that prompts the leader to consider the next steps required to enhance organizational performance.[146] The S-Curve has been used across organizational types, e.g., the author has used it in industrial and administrative functions to amplify performance within existing resources. Simply stated the S-Curve approach drives leadership to always be in beta mode as today's level of performance is viewed as the transition point to the higher levels of performance within the same, or less, resources. This introduction links the S-Curve to gaining and sustaining a future orientation as a leader; once understood and applied it becomes almost impossible

---

144 Dan Wellers and Kai Goerlich, "The Human Factor in an AI Future," SAP Insights, July, 21, 2021, The Human Factor in an AI Future | SAP Insights.

145 Vermeulen, "Lights Out."

146 Shohreh Ghorbani, "The Philosophy behind S-Curves," YouTube, 2017, https://www.youtube.com/watch?v=2s6SEYvRdvc&list=PLI-qstduR-XY-47y2x4CUZDeh0uiodqPJn.

to avoid its application. The S-Curve philosophy serves as an antecedent to change and innovation.[147]

FUTURE SCENARIOS INSTEAD OF STATUS QUO

The status quo, with all its quirks and concerns, is typically more comfortable for most players because it is a known entity;[148] the mere possibility of change creates anxiety and fear as people consider what may be lost and what they may have to do differently – the fear of carnage accompanies change.[149] A critical leader attribute is recognizing and accepting this natural fear of change while balancing it with the need to anticipate the future.[150] If the concepts above are adopted, i.e., self-reflection, environmental scanning, constant learning, and use of the S-Curve technique, the leader is poised to consider not just the future but multiple different future scenarios that provide the organization multiple avenues of approach to future viability and success.[151] It is this willingness to learn and explore options that provides the leader with a future orientation, an orientation that is deliberate and always under development.[152]

---

147 Aubrey C. Daniels, *Performance Management: Changing Behavior That Drives Organizational Effectiveness* (Atlanta, GA: Performance Management Publications, 2014).

148 Gary Hammel, *Leading the Revolution: How to Thrive in Turbulent Times by making Innovation a Way of Life* (Boston, MA: Penguin Books, Ltd, 2002).

149 Stanleigh, "Effecting Successful Change Management Initiatives."

150 Giuseppe Santisi, Ernesto Lodi, Paola Magnano, Rita Zarbo, and Andrea Zammitti, "Relationship between Psychological Capital and Quality of Life: The Role of Courage," *Sustainability* 12, no. 13 (2020): 5238, https://doi.org/10.3390/su12135238.

151 Chermack, *Scenario Planning*.

152 Ibid.

SUMMARY

- The old axiom that failing to plan is planning to fail is germane to having a future orientation. The plan may fail but the thinking behind it will serve you well.
- There is no one way to look at the future; if actively considered and pursued multiple future scenarios exist.
- Active learning and the use of future-oriented techniques such as self-reflection and the S-Curve help ingrain a future orientation.
- The future can be shaped and is much closer than most think.

Section II. People

People reflect the wildcard for organizational leaders. This remains true even as many organizations indicate people are their most important resource. Until the fully automated dark factory arrives there is no escaping this simple point.[153]

In contemporary organizations, leaders face a kaleidoscope of people issues as individuals, subgroups, and groups have differing cultures, different values, and different expectations of the organization.[154] One sees this complexity in the conflicts underway between political parties, religions, and within the domain of identity politics. Leaders cannot escape this complexity. With every interaction the kaleidoscope can change; leaders are not on firm ground in the people area, so special considerations and skills are needed to augment the leader's technical proficiency within the work area.[155]

The chapters following speak to the critical elements of influencing[156] people to do good work every day with an umbrella caveat that leaders must understand - the

---

153   Vermeulen, "Lights Out."
154   Vernon K. Robbins, Exploring the Texture of Texts: A Guide to Socio-Rhetorical Interpretation (New York, NY: Bloomsbury Publishing Plc, 2012).
155   Northouse, *Leadership*.
156   Cialdini, *Influence*.

culture of the organization trumps all else.[157] Leaders must have a deep understanding of the cultures within business units and other organizational groupings as the leader engages the environment and seeks success. Culture runs deep; it is reflected in the organization's DNA.[158] As leaders attempt change efforts the culture will push back.[159] Leaders must understand this given the failure rate of change efforts.[160]

The paragraphs above sound negative. They are not meant to be. Simply realistic. Leaders have a complex task relative to people management. Leaders must focus on gaining and increasing trust with the people within the organization and the organization's external stakeholders: Trust is the super glue that will allow leaders to positively leverage the skills, competencies, and talents of the people element within the organization.[161] Trust is gained through relationships.[162] Relationship management thus becomes a leader competency in high demand; cultivating, developing, and sustaining relationships becomes paramount for leaders at all levels within the organization.[163] Many will recoil here, but this includes with those individuals that leaders consider their most negative, least desirable members, or what in an Air Force depot were

---

157 Edgar H. Schein, Organizational Culture and Leadership (New Jersey: Wiley, 2016).
158 Geert Hofstede, Gert Jan Hofstede, and Michael Minkov, *Cultures and Organizations: Software of the Mind: Intercultural Cooperation and Its Importance for Survival* (Johanneshov: Mtm, 2017).
159 Oster, "Listening to Luddites."
160 Stanleigh, "Effecting Successful Change Management Initiatives."
161 Simoes et al., "Improving Change Management."
162 Ibid.
163 Sin et al., "Understanding Why They Don't See Eye to Eye."

called POS (pieces of sh!t).[164] In reality, these folks, often found among the unengaged or the actively disengaged populations of the workforce, can be among the most valuable of all organizational members. As a leader you should never avoid[165] these people but instead actively listen to their questions and concerns; resistance can often be misperceived as the employee or team may simply be processing the change and seeking to understand.[166] This process of active listening, addressing questions and concerns, and seeking to help those in the throes of change critically think through the process of change is referred to as Discovery Learning.[167] As a leader you should be a master of this concept as you seek to improve organizational effectiveness as Discovery Learning is a persuasion and guiding technique to re-socialize historical behaviors.[168] The high cost of recruiting, onboarding, assimilating, and, if necessary, terminating employees demands that you engage every employee; no employee should be allowed to remain unengaged or actively disengaged. This is a failure of leadership as you, the leader, are responsible for the overall work environment.[169] Starting today you should engage every single person to improve your organizational effectiveness.

---

164 Oster, "Listening to Luddites."

165 Katz and Flynn, "Understanding Conflict Management Systems."

166 Mattias Georg Will and Ingo Pies, "Sensemaking and Sensegiving," *Journal of Accounting & Organizational Change* 14, no. 3 (2018): 291-313, https://doi.org/10.1108/jaoc-11-2016-0075.

167 HeeKap Lee, "Jesus Teaching Through Discovery," *International Christian Community of Teacher Educators Journal* 1, no. 2 (2006).

168 Lee, "Jesus Teaching Through Discovery."

169 Elizabeth Dukes, "The Employee Experience: What It Is and Why It Matters," Inc.com, August 31, 2017, https://www.inc.com/elizabeth-dukes/the-employee-experience-what-it-is-and-why-it-matt.html.

Leading people is complex. Special considerations and competencies are required; however, this complexity can be simplified, and effectiveness increased if you accept that every interaction is both a negotiation[170] and a fresh start in maintaining high-quality relationships.[171] The simplicity of these approaches can be startling yet most every kid is taught this…use the Golden Rule in every interaction even if conflict and high stress are underway.[172] The following three chapters speak to different aspects of leading people. The key learning point is to remember addressing emotions first is a requirement – only after the emotional aspects of issues are addressed can the rational, logical concerns be successful.[173] Knowing your audience is paramount.[174]

SUMMARY

- Remember the kaleidoscope analogy; people's emotions, and in many cases sense of identity, change ergo their behavior changes…sometimes instantly… understand this as a both risk and opportunity.
- Culture rules: This is a repetitive theme through-out this book.
- Trust makes or breaks organizations. It is the super-glue of high-quality relationships.
- The Golden Rule is applicable in every interaction.

---

170 Cialdini, *Influence*.
171 LeBlanc and Gonzalez-Roma, "LMX."
172 Katz and Flynn, "Understanding Conflict Management Systems."
173 John Baldoni, *Great Communication Secrets of Great Leaders* (New York, NY: McGraw-Hill Education – Europe, 2003).
174 Udayar et al., "Emotional Intelligence and Performance."

Chapter 3. The Power of Leader Engagement

"Concentrate all your thoughts on the task at hand. The sun's rays do not burn until brought to focus".[175]

"Remember that a person's name is to that person the sweetest and most important sound in any language".[176]

The long-term historical data indicate an incredibly high number of disengaged or actively disengaged people in the global workforce with only 13 – 20 percent of employees engaged.[177] Similar data depict that over half the workforce is unhappy, do not trust their leadership team, and are not motivated by the organization's mission, assuming the mission is known.[178] This phenomenon exists even as large numbers of organizations proclaim

---

[175] Alexander Grahan Bell, "Alexander Graham Bell Quotes," BrainyQuote.com, 2021, Alexander Graham Bell - Concentrate all your thoughts upon... (brainyquote.com).

[176] Dale Carnegie, "Inspiring Quotes by Dale Carnegie," Optimize, 2021, "Remember that a person's name is to that person the sweetest sound and most important sound in any language." | Optimize.

[177] Lawrence, "What are the Causes & Nature of Employee Disengagement?"

[178] Ibid.

people are the organization's most valuable resource.[179] The percent of engaged employees may ebb and flow; however, the astute leader immediately sees that minimally 80 percent of salary and benefits are for naught. Worse, recruiting, onboarding, and terminating employees can be an unrecognized cost while, conversely, maintaining these employees is a known detriment to organizational performance.[180]

Numerous globally famous organizations have addressed low employee engagement with surveys, action plans, leader coaching certifications, and a myriad of other improvement offerings yet the trend persists. Something is missing from the cookie cutter approach to addressing the phenomenon. The author is firmly convinced that low employee engagement is a symptom of low leader engagement, a term not often used to define the root cause of this phenomenon. The author's perspective is grounded in the simple fact that the leader is responsible for the organizational climate and the overall employee experience;[181] if trust is an issue then the leader has the onus, the burden, to negate this issue.[182] If true, then the issue of employee engagement needs to be readdressed as leader engagement. The following sections are offered as means to understanding leader engagement as a foundational issue to higher levels of employee commitment and organizational effectiveness.

---

179 Debashis Chatterjee, "Wise Ways: Leadership as Relationship," *Journal of Human Values* 12, no. 2 (2006): 153-160, https://doi.org/10.1177/097168580601200204.

180 Lawrence, "What are the Causes & Nature of Employee Disengagement?"

181 Dukes, "The Employee Experience."

182 Simoes et al., "Improving Change Management."

EMOTIONAL INTELLIGENCE'S RELATIONSHIP MANAGEMENT

As introduced earlier EI is the recognition of how emotion and feelings intersect and interplay within the performance domain.[183] Many in leadership shy away from the touchy-feely aspects of emotion yet it is a critical variable in understanding relationships given leaders invariably evoke a range of emotions with every single interaction between and among organizational members and stakeholders.[184] The regularity of this emotive impact may not be consciously recognized to the detriment of the organization as the dynamics of EI cascade and ripple throughout the organization.[185] The classic example of leadership causing emotion is the anxiety and stress that results from a leader who is always reactive, typically running around with his/her hair on fire – this is the person followers want gone. There is a gross distinction between having a sense of urgency and being totally out of control.[186]

From the EI perspective relationship management addresses the leader's ability to directly influence[187] and manage the emotions of others within the organization.[188] Leadership effectiveness in this regard can be reflected by the ability to establish collective goals and objectives; the recognition by members of the importance of the

---

183 Antonakis et al., "Does Leadership Need Emotional Intelligence?"
184 Shelley Thompkins, *Leaders Level of Emotional Intelligence and Its Influence on Employee Engagement: A Case Study* (PhD diss., Capella University, 2015).
185 Udayar et al., "Emotional Intelligence and Performance."
186 Ibid.
187 Cialdini, *Influence*.
188 Smith, "Enhancing Your Emotional Intelligence."

organization's work; successfully cultivating and sustaining enthusiasm, cooperation, and trust; and gaining acceptance of change and innovation.[189] From this perspective it becomes easier to see the intersection between relationship management and employee engagement which has been defined as the employee's mental state relative to the organization's effectiveness[190] – the two are directly related.[191] This intersection will be addressed in more detail in Chapter 4, High-Quality Relationships; however, before we explore relationships from a theoretical perspective we must understand more about leadership engagement from the member or stakeholder perspective.

UNDER THE MICROSCOPE

A common theme about the employee experience[192] is that employees leave the organization due to bad managers.[193] As a leader you are always being observed by organizational members and, for better or for worse, many model your behavior. If negativity is your norm then negativity typically encapsulates and exudes from the work environment as negative behaviors are the norm.[194] It is this mirroring or mimicry that underlies the military approach to leadership wherein the leader is expected

---

189 Antonakis et al. "Does Leadership Need Emotional Intelligence?"
190 Thompkins, "Leaders Level of Emotional Intelligence."
191 Antonakis et al., "Does Leadership Need Emotional Intelligence?"
192 Lawrence, "What are the Causes & Nature of Employee Disengagement?"
193 Thompkins, "Leaders Level of Emotional Intelligence."
194 Galit Meisler, Amos Drory, and Eran Vigoda-Gadot, "Perceived Organizational Politics and Counterproductive Work Behavior: The Mediating Role of Hostility," *Personnel Review* 49, no. 8 (2019): 1505-1517, https://doi.org/10.1108/pr-12-2017-0392.

to set the example, to literally walk the talk of leadership by being calm under fire, of demeanor, attitude, competence, and approachability.[195] The military is imperfect yet the expectation is enforced as commanders and other levels of leadership are routinely relieved if the climate and/or performance expectations are not met. No one ever speaks to the burden of followership.

HUMILITY – IT IS HARD TO BE HUMBLE

Humility is directly linked to EI's self-awareness component[196] and is an easily discernible trait for organizational members and stakeholders to determine. For many leaders it is next to impossible to be humble given the status, perks, and power of their position;[197] however, humbleness is an antecedent to high-quality relationships and amplified organizational performance that leaders should ponder.[198] Humility sends the message that the leader is not only approachable but is likely to have mastered the nuances of bias and tolerance of others, or, respectively, intellectual humility and cultural humility.[199]

The two perspectives on humility are worthy of deeper exploration due to the simple fact the humble leader is better postured to interact with a globally diverse

---

195 United States, Department of the Army, *Army Leadership: Competent, Confident, and Agile*, Washington, DC, HQ, Dept. of the Army, 2006.
196 Smith, "Enhancing Your Emotional Intelligence."
197 Drew, "Enabling or "Real" Power and Influence in Leadership."
198 Daryl R. Van Tongeren, Don E. Davis, Joshua N. Hook, and Charlotte vanOyen Witvliet, "Humility," *Current Directions in Psychological Science* 28, no. 5 (2019): 463-468. https://doi.org/10.1177/096372149850153.
199 Van Tongeren et al., "Humility."

environment than is an arrogant leader.[200] The intellectually humble leader is recognized as being attuned to his/her own beliefs and values but cognizant that respect of others is necessary – the beliefs and values of others are not disregarded or disrespected.[201] Similarly, the culturally humble leader portrays an openness and a willingness to learn about other cultures.[202] The dichotomy, again, links directly to EI in that humility overlays the four components, i.e., self-awareness, self-management, social awareness, and relationship management,[203] and directly impacts the quality of leader member relationships.[204]

A key learning point infers that humility helps the leader build the social bonds necessary to amplify organization effectiveness given the inevitability that the leader will encounter failure, the leader will need help, the leader will create negative emotions due to the requirement to make decisions that do not include everyone's input, and the leader will eventually need to repair damaged relationships. Humility can be both the glue to strengthen relationships and the oil to reduce the friction that naturally occurs within dynamic, diverse organizations as humble leaders, even in the midst of stress, retain better relational characteristics – people are more apt to assist and forgive the humble leader.[205] The comparison to the hard-charging, self-centered leader does not have to occur - no words are necessary; most everyone has

---

200 Ibid.
201 Van Tongeren et al., "Humility."
202 Ibid.
203 Smith, "Enhancing Your Emotional Intelligence."
204 LeBlanc and Gonzalez-Roma, "LMX."
205 Van Tongeren et al., "Humility."

seen or been part of the collateral damage done by this type leader.

COMMON COURTESY DRAWS A CROWD

Dale Carnegie recognized a long time ago that people react positively to hearing their name.[206] Napoleon, even longer ago, spoke to the power of recognition as a means to enhance performance.[207] Saying someone's name is the most basic form of recognition. Every person, regardless of level within the organization, is worthy of recognition and should be recognized or acknowledged unless doing so creates a hazard or unsafe condition. If the person's name is unknown the leader should minimally make eye contact and extend a greeting. There absolutely are situations in which the leader may be forced to forgo this recognition or acknowledgement, e.g., to comply with varying cultural norms;[208] however, if the leader has a history of this type of positive engagement people will understand the situational requirements. People will also understand if the leader's history is one of aloofness, arrogance, or only engaging when in need – this speaks directly to authenticity as people are very quick, very adept at identifying the falsity of this approach.[209]

---

206 Carnegie, "Inspiring Quotes."
207 Napolean Bonaparte, "A Soldier Will Fight Long and Hard for a Bit of Colored Ribbon," BrainyQuote.com, (n.d.) Napoleon Bonaparte - A soldier will fight long and hard... (brainyquote.com).
208 Hofstede et al., "Cultures and Organizations: Software of the Mind."
209 Northouse, *Leadership*.

The need for civility is high in the contemporary environment;[210] the leader focused on organization effectiveness will understand the power of this approach to enhance a positive employee experience.[211]

SUMMARY

- Leader Engagement is required to negate low Employee Engagement.
- Humility enhances relationships.
- Greet or acknowledge everyone when possible.
- Civility and common courtesy should be the norm.

---

210 Deborah L. Center, "Three as of Civility: Acknowledgment, Authentic Conversations, and Action," *The Journal of Continuing Education in Nursing* 41, no. 11 (2010): 488-489, https://doi.org/10.3928/00220124-20101026-04.

211 Dukes, "The Employee Experience: What It Is and Why It Matters."

Chapter 4. High-Quality Relationships

"It is surprising how much you can accomplish if you don't care who gets the credit".[212]

People. The Human Element. An organization's most important resource. An organization's most problematic resource. If only leaders did not have to deal with people. Until Artificial Intelligence replaces the human element[213] woe unto the leader who does not attempt to understand the power and pitfalls of relationships.[214]

In the years before 2020 the author used the word vortex to describe the contemporary operating environment, the dawn of a new era, as leaders faced the confluence of the growing influence of Artificial Intelligence and technology in the workplace,[215] the dissolution of

---

212 Lee Colan, "12 Quotes to help You build More Powerful Relationships," Inc.com, March 30, 2016, 12 Quotes to Help You Build More Powerful Relationships | Inc.com.
213 Vermeulen, "Lights Out."
214 A. Newman, G. Schwarz, B. Cooper, and S. Sendjaya, "How Servant Leadership Influences Organizational Citizenship Behavior: The Roles of LMX, Empowerment, and Proactive Personality," *Journal of Business Ethics* 145, no. 1 (2017): 49-62, https://doi.org/10.1007/s10551-015-2827-6.
215 Xin Li, Qianqian Xie, Jiaojiao Jiang, Yuan Zhou, and Lucheng Huang, "Identifying and Monitoring the Development of Trends of Emerging Technologies Using Patent Analysis and Twitter Data Mining: The Case of Perovskite Solar Cell Technology," *Technological Forecasting & Social Change* 146, (2019): 687-705, https://doi.org/10.1016/j.techfore.2018.06.004.

Western liberal democracy,[216] the oft avoided growth of Islamic influence in Western societies,[217] and generic immigration/migration considerations, among other geopolitical issues, as organizational decisions were made. The pandemic intensified the vortex by exacerbating the issues and speeding the pace of technological change underway. In effect, the pandemic brought forth differing visions of the near future that exacerbated both organizational direction and human element concerns.[218]

Relational issues are of increasingly paramount concern as the near future arrives on unstable, shifting ground. The need for clear vision and purpose is manifest even as the volatility and ambiguity of this uncertain environment continues to create chaos, anxiety, and in many cases carnage as the changes unfold.[219] If people are truly an organization's most important resource, then relationship management is a required leader competency.

RELATIONSHIP MANAGEMENT

The basic EI approach to relationship management is emotive, i.e., managing the emotions of others;[220] however, a deeper dive into this concept indicates leaders must be aware of the affective, behavioral, and cognitive

---

[216] Peter Hille and Christoph Hasselbach, "Capitol Hill Riots: Are Western Democracies under Attack?" dw.com, 2021, Capitol Hill riots: Are Western democracies under attack? (msn.com).

[217] Alan Lake, "Tipping Point for Islamic Domination = 20% of Population," 4freedoms.com, 2015, http://4freedoms.com/video/how-islam-is-taking-over-the-world-islamization-explained.

[218] David Brubaker, Cinnie Noble, Richard Fincher, Susan K. Park, and Sharon Press, "Conflict Resolution in the Workplace: What Will the Future Bring?" *Conflict Resolution Quarterly* 31, no. 4 (2014): 357-386, https://doi.org/10.1002/crq.21104.

[219] Stanleigh, "Effecting Successful Change Management Initiatives."

[220] Smith, "Enhancing Your Emotional Intelligence."

aspects of the human element to gain not only trust but performance well beyond contractual levels which should be every leader's goal.[221] Critically, the term affective addresses a person's moods, feelings, and attitudes each of which impacts the organization minute by minute. Every leader interaction, whether consciously or unconsciously, simultaneously is impacted by these three elements while also causing impact. These are the interwoven and complex aspects of relationship management that leaders should have cognizance as every interaction is a communication that both influences and persuades for better or for worse.[222] In essence, the affective, behavioral, and cognitive characteristics become the individual's personality. Leaders can leverage this knowledge using assessments to better understand and anticipate how individuals likely will relate and react to interactions.

PERSONALITY ASSESSMENTS

The intent of this section is not to recommend any one assessment but to highlight how the leader can leverage the assessment outcomes to better relate to individuals. Many organizations seek to treat all employees the same to avoid litigation or other controversies, yet this often fails simply because every person is unique. The key is to treat every person with dignity and respect simply to recognize their value as a person[223] while acknowledging the person's basic personality traits, e.g., introverted or

---

221 Simoes et al., "Improving Change Management."
222 Ibid.
223 Abad Ahmad, "Management by Human Values: An Overview," *Journal of Human Values* 5, no. 1 (1999): 15-23, https://doi.org/10.1177/097168589900500103.

extroverted, and his/her strengths.[224] It is often overlooked but elemental that an introverted person may internalize whereas the extroverted person may very quickly verbalize concern as they engage in sensemaking.[225] The unskilled leader likely will miss opportunities to better relate and to cultivate high-quality relationships due to these miscues in reading the environment.[226] There is both art and science involved in this aspect of leader engagement as the leader may adjust the interactive approach dependent upon the unique differences between and among individuals – knowing yourself and knowing the people that report to you is fundamental to leadership.[227]

PERFORMANCE MANAGEMENT

Regardless of personality type or set of strengths every person needs to understand how his/her assignment relates to other members of the team or group and how individual performance ultimately aligns to the organization's vision and goals.[228] In the author's experience this linear function does not always occur which leads invariably to friction.[229] This orientation, or lack thereof, will be the first of many communications that the organizational members use to gauge the effectiveness of the leader.[230]

---

224 Buckingham and Clifton, *Now Discover Your Strengths*.
225 Will and Pies, "Sensemaking and Sensegiving."
226 Sin et al., "Understanding Why They Don't See Eye to Eye."
227 United States, *Army Leadership: Competent, Confident, and Agile*.
228 James M. Kouzes and Barry Z. Posner, *The Leadership Challenge: How to Make Extraordinary Things Happen in Organizations* (San Francisco, CA: Jossey-Bass, 2012).
229 Sin et al., "Understanding Why They Don't See Eye to Eye."
230 LeBlanc and Gonzalez-Roma, "LMX."

A secondary issue for leaders to understand is the importance of in- and out-groups within the organization.[231] This grouping will occur unless the leader consciously engages every employee with the deliberate intent to cultivate, develop, and sustain a high-quality relationship.[232] This may be an unpleasant undesirable requirement given the employee and the environment but unless done the organization will suffer from low employee engagement which the author considers a symptom of poor leader engagement.[233] The leader should anticipate this type grouping and make every practicable effort to negate this phenomenon from occurring.[234]

Performance is adversely impacted if trust does not exist,[235] or stated differently, trust is an antecedent to performance beyond contractual levels,[236] e.g., micromanagement is a trust killer given the employee never attains even contractual levels of performance under this leadership engagement approach.[237] Trust thus becomes an intangible commodity that eludes most in leadership if the global history of low employee engagement is the lagging indicator.[238] This intangible, trust, leads us to the underlying theories in play as leaders consciously engage in relationship management.[239]

---

231 Northouse, *Leadership*.
232 Ibid.
233 Thompkins, *Leaders Level of Emotional Intelligence*.
234 Sin et al., "Understanding Why They Don't See Eye to Eye."
235 Ibid.
236 Daniels, *Performance Management*.
237 Sosik and Jung, Full Range Leadership Development.
238 Dukes, "The Employee Experience."
239 Smith, "Enhancing Your Emotional Intelligence."

THEORY BEHIND PRACTICE

The primary relationship-oriented theory is leader member exchange (LMX) theory.[240] At a high level and in its most simple form LMX theory addresses the one-to-one relationship between leader and member (follower, employee, etc.) and the quality thereof.[241] If the relationship is high-quality the member invariably will belong to the in-group. Conversely, if the relationship is poor, the member will default to the out-group.[242] This in- and out-group association directly relates to the member's affective commitment to the leader and ultimately to the organization.[243] Critically, LMX is directly related to organization performance and effectiveness; relationships matter.[244] The LMX theory is the pinnacle, actually the blending, of two supporting theories, i.e., social exchange theory and role theory. These two will be summarized before LMX theory is discussed in more detail.

Role Theory

Role theory addresses the science behind a person entering an organization and the steps taken from onboarding to contract level performance or discretionary effort, a level of effort which comes with high-quality relationships.[245] Role theory identifies a 3-step process each member faces as he/she is assimilated into the organization. If the member does not reach the third step then he/

---
240 Northouse, *Leadership*.
241 Graen and Uhl-Bien, "Relationship-Based Approach to Leadership."
242 Northouse, *Leadership*.
243 LeBlanc and Gonzalez-Roma, "LMX."
244 Ibid.
245 Schriesheim et al., "LMX."

she very probably will never join the leader's in-group.[246] In some research these three steps have been named Stranger, Acquaintance, and Partner to quickly reflect the level of relationship.[247]

Upon onboarding the member assumes the first step, the Stranger phase, which is role making. In this step the member is learning the organization as well as gauging the leader, i.e., is the leader perceived as a threat or someone who is willing to assist the member as well as making discernments relative to the leader's competence. This occurs simultaneously with the leader gauging the new member's attitudes, behaviors, willingness to learn, and receptiveness to guidance. Work is at or near the contractual or job description level and the interaction is more one wherein the leader defines expectations; the member is in receive mode with little, if any, influence.[248]

With time and learning the member begins to assume the role making Acquaintance stage which is the make-or-break point for establishing high quality relationships.[249] Exchanges between the leader and member are increasing, the leader has begun to allocate resources required for success, and the mutual assessment has intensified. If the parties begin social exchanges and the comfort between the two increases, trust begins to emerge. It is this salient point, the emergence of trust, that determines whether the member stays in the role

---

246 Ibid.
247 Graen and Uhl-Bien, "Relationship-Based Approach to Leadership."
248 Katherine M. Kelley and Ryan S. Bisel, "Leaders' Narrative Sensemaking During LMX Role Negotiations: Explaining How Leaders Make Sense of Who to Trust and When," *The Leadership Quarterly* 25, (2014): 433-448, http://dx.doi.org/10.1016/j.leaqua.2013.10.011.
249 Graen and Uhl-Bien, "Relationship-Based Approach to Leadership."

making step or enters role routinization.[250] In role making the communication exchanges refine, perhaps redefine, the members role as the parties interact.[251]

Within role routinization or the Partnership stage, social exchanges are frequent; trust, respect, and mutual obligation abound; resources become more readily available to the member as do new opportunities; and member performance is well beyond contractual or job description level as the member's affective commitment to the organization is reflected by the member readily identifying with the organization.[252] The member is solidly within the in-group[253] as trust, respect, and mutual obligation are expansive. The organization reaps the benefit of these high-quality relationships.[254]

If the social exchanges between leader and member remain minimal, comfort between the two remains questionable, and performance does not begin to exceed contractual or job description levels the member will not attain role routinization or in-group status.[255] It is at this Acquaintance stage that both leader and follower are trying to make sense of the value of the relationship; if either deems the relationship to be of little to no value or the other player to be untrustworthy then the requisite social exchanges will not occur; the member typically reverts to the Stranger stage with contract level performance the

---

250 Schriesheim et al., "LMX."
251 Kelly and Bisel, "Leaders' Narrative Sensemaking."
252 Schriesheim et al., "LMX."
253 Northouse, *Leadership*.
254 Graen and Uhl-Bien, "Relationship-Based Approach to Leadership."
255 Schriesheim et al., "LMX."

norm[256] and the member excluded from the in-group.[257] This is often referred to as office politics and favoritism; however, both parties are initially responsible if truth be told even as subsequent tension and conflict emerge.[258]

A critical learning point is that all leaders naturally differentiate between and among members based upon the social exchanges that occur within role negotiations, i.e., leaders, by default, respond differently to individual members if not consciously aware of the behind-the-scenes interplay between and among personalities and relationship management.[259] A second learning point is the "how to" cultivate, sustain, and develop relationships is a learnable skill ergo all members are potential Partners.[260]

Of note, this 3-Step role process is an on-going negotiation that occurs with every interaction as the parties seek trust which is very simply a mutual determination as to the other party's reliability.[261] These negotiations are the social exchanges which will be addressed below.

Social Exchange Theory

At its essence social exchange theory is summarized by the "what's in it for me" or WIIFM question. Social exchanges begin in the Stranger stage via contractual

---

[256] Kelly and Bisel, "Leaders' Narrative Sensemaking."

[257] Northouse, *Leadership*.

[258] Rachel Singleton, Leslie A. Toombs, Sonia Taneja, Charlotte Larkin, and Mildred Golden Pryor, "Workplace Conflict: A Strategic Leadership Imperative," *International Journal of Business & Public Administration* 8, no. 1 (2011): 149-163.

[259] Graen and Uhl-Bien, "Relationship-Based Approach to Leadership."

[260] Ibid.

[261] Kelly and Bisel, "Leaders' Narrative Sensemaking."

level expectation learning, initial assignments and reviews, and the beginning of resource exchanges, e.g., the leader publicly recognizing the member's accession to the organization, training opportunities, etc. These exchanges are initially transactional in nature simply due to the member's newness to the organization and the expectation of contractual level performance; resourcing is the currency involved in each transaction while trustworthiness and reliability are the measures of success.[262]

In high-quality relationships the social exchanges exceed mere contractual transactional levels as the individual moves beyond the WIIFM attitude to a more organizational-centric perspective as loyalty and commitment increase.[263] As social exchanges reach the Partnership stage the member begins to identify with the organization to the point of an emotional sense of belonging with pride of membership the norm. This sense of affective commitment increases as the member's sense of affiliation, esteem, and emotional support increase.[264] This affective commitment is the antecedent to discretionary effort which drives numerous positive benefits to the organization, e.g., members within the role routinization stage typically are not hesitant to put the organization before self and engaging in other voluntary behaviors such as knowledge sharing.[265]

---

262 Kelly and Bisel, "Leaders' Narrative Sensemaking."
263 Qi Hao, Yijun Shi, and Weiguo Yang, "How Leader-Member Exchange Affects Knowledge Sharing Behavior: Understanding the Effects of Commitment and Employee Characteristics," *Frontiers in Psychology* 10, (2019), https://doi.org/10.3389/fpsyg.2019.02768.
264 Hao et al., "How LMX Affects Knowledge Sharing."
265 Ibid.

Leader Member Exchange Theory

The LMX theory is applicable to leader member dyads, the one-to-one relationships, as well as leader group and leader network systems.[266] It captures the essence of leadership which has never been universally defined[267] but which implicitly contains three domains: the leader, the follower, and the relationship.[268] As discussed above high-quality relationships benefit the actors as well as the organization and relationship management is a learnable skill that amplifies performance.[269] Given the three domains LMX theory arguably underlies all other leadership theories as it is foundational.[270] It defines the power of relationships relative to organizational effectiveness thus establishing relationships as the cornerstone to negating low employee engagement. The onus is on leaders to engage which requires a deep understanding of the organizational culture to anticipate resistance and challenges to establishing high-quality relationships as the norm.[271]

Leadership is a System

The three subsections immediately above speak to one aspect of leadership as a system. The scope of this book disallows a comprehensive review of this concept but the key components are the leader, the follower,

---

266 Northhouse, *Leadership*.
267 Ibid.
268 Graen and Uhl-Bien, "Relationship-Based Approach to Leadership."
269 Ibid.
270 Newman et al., "How Servant Leadership Influences Organizational Citizenship Behavior."
271 Oster, "Listening to Luddites."

and the situation over time.[272] The subsections above infer this system dynamic[273] via addressing Leadership Engagement and the author's belief that Emotional Intelligence is a key tool in leveraging the power of relationships in any situation.[274] If the leader is attuned to relationship management then, from a systems perspective, the opportunity exists to create and sustain a powerful positive reinforcing loop[275] that gains the organization sustained trust and affective commitment, the key drivers for high performance and amplified organizational effectiveness.[276]

A key learning point is that the leader should understand the two-way dynamics of traits (who the actors are) simply because cognition (how the actors think), affect (how the actors feel), and behavior (what the actors do) are critical variables in every relationship[277] and impact whether the member is viewed as a stranger, acquaintance, or a partner – a perspective which ultimately impacts organizational performance.[278] Of concern this member perspective can be expanded to include malefactor or enemy if the leader considers the impact of a member who is actively disengaged which adds more tension and stress to the relational concerns.[279]

---

272 Sosik and Jung, *Full Range Leadership Development*.
273 Meadows, *Leverage Points*.
274 Thompkins, *Leaders Level of Emotional Intelligence*.
275 Donella H. Meadows, *Dancing with Systems: An Excerpt from her Unfinished Manuscript Thinking in Systems* (Whole Earth Review, 58-63).
276 Sosik and Jung, *Full Range Leadership Development*.
277 Ibid.
278 Sin et al., "Understanding Why They Don't See Eye to Eye."
279 Buckingham and Clifton, *Now Discover Your Strengths*.

This intersection of dynamic relational variables and of relational perspectives is a leverage point[280] for the leader astute in the nuances of leadership style and performance results, e.g., the micromanager loses member trust and performance due to intimidation and fear while the inspirational leader increases trust, affective commitment, and high performance for the organization.[281] This relational intersection plays out at every organizational level[282] as the actors engage in sense-giving and sensemaking,[283] i.e., the effort to both understand the interaction and to determine the other's trustworthiness.[284] At a more macro level the organization's environment comes into play during these interactions, or more succinctly, the organization's culture.[285]

CULTURE DOMINATES: DIGNITY AND RESPECT

Culture, like leadership, has never been universally defined[286] yet it is imminently powerful, and if not intentionally influenced by the leader, may not allow the organization to adapt to desired change and innovation.[287] Culture may also be so toxic that employees cannot perform ergo the need for the leader to understand and

---

280 Meadows, *Leverage Points*.
281 Sosik and Jung, *Full Range Leadership Development*.
282 Ibid.
283 Will and Pies, "Sensemaking and Sensegiving."
284 Kelly and Bisel, "Leaders' Narrative Sensemaking."
285 Kim S. Cameron and Robert Quinn, *Diagnosing and Changing Organizational Culture: Based on the Competing Values Framework* (San Francisco, CA: Jossey-Bass, 2011).
286 Northouse, *Leadership*.
287 Schein, *Organizational Culture and Leadership*.

deliberately apply the concept of employee experience.[288] If leaders condone the in- and out-group phenomenon's existence[289] then leadership should not be surprised or angered by the resulting friction within the workplace as these groups naturally react to various levels of performance, opportunities to grow, and the perception of favoritism.[290] Worse, this phenomenon results in the use of adjectives such as Luddites[291] or POS to describe employees in the out-group who do not mesh well and who may well be actively attempting to destroy the organization.[292] This type conflict and divisive behavior must not be condoned or allowed to become part of the culture at any level.[293] And, as the author has personally witnessed, at no time should a leader name call any member: Every person has the right to be treated with dignity and respect regardless of group.[294]

The topic of culture *per se* exceeds the parameters of this work yet should be an area in which the leader is competent;[295] if not, then the leader may be clueless why desired changes fail.[296] Succinctly, if the desired change does not fit the culture then the idea will ultimately fail

---

[288] Dukes, "The Employee Experience."
[289] Northouse, *Leadership*.
[290] Sin et al., "Understanding Why They Don't See Eye to Eye."
[291] Oster, "Listening to Luddites."
[292] Buckingham and Clifton, *Now Discover Your Strengths*.
[293] Schein, *Organizational Culture and Leadership*.
[294] Chatterjee, "Wise Ways."
[295] Tony Carter, "Global Leadership," *Journal of Management Policy and Practice* 14, no. 1 (2013): 69-74.
[296] Stanleigh, "Effecting Successful Change Management Initiatives."

mid- to long-term.[297] Until the dark factory subsumes the organization[298] the social tendencies of the human element will pervade the organization, i.e., the organization is a community, a living organism,[299] that will have a dominant culture as well as an innate sense of character and identity.[300] The dominate culture will ultimately reject change efforts that do not fit this sense of character and identity hence the need for leadership to know the culture thoroughly as culture is more powerful than strategy or any other management system.[301] Let that sink in. The dominate organizational culture, for better or for worse, will reject strategies and other change interventions that do not align.[302] The author often witnessed this in military organizations that overtly adapted superficially to new commanders but at the deeper levels of culture never changed due to the commanders' relatively short tenure – the organization could simply await the commander's departure knowing deep enduring change would not occur.[303]

Leaders entering a new organization should be acutely aware of culture's pervasive power and should be prepared to adapt their leadership style to the new

---

297 William E. Schneider, "Why Good Management Ideas Fail: The Neglected Power of Organizational Culture," *Strategy & Leadership* 28, no. 1 (2000): 24-29, https://doi.org/10.1108/10878570010336001.
298 Vermeulen, "Lights Out."
299 Morgan, *Images of Organizations*.
300 Schneider, "Why Good Management Ideas Fail."
301 Ibid.
302 Ibid.
303 Schein, *Organizational Culture and Leadership*.

environment if success is desired,[304] e.g., a control-oriented leader will likely struggle in a collaborative culture[305] without intentionally adapting to the new culture and adopting a more collaborative style.[306] Recognizing the dominate cultural type is a critical leader competency;[307] however, culture is even more complicated because every society, whether localized to a group within an organization or from a nation-to-nation comparison,[308] has differing dimensions[309] that must also be understood to dampen the potential for conflict[310] and to posture the leader for success.[311]

Specific to this work the author's intent is to simply link relationship management to culture to ensure the reader recognizes the need to ponder the intersection of this set of powerful dynamics within every organization. Relationship management and culture can be linked to create or design a very positive employee experience that amplifies goodness throughout the organization.[312] This is a leadership opportunity[313] that can be accomplished via

---

[304] Richard M. Steers, Carlos Sanchez-Runde, and Luciara Nardon, "Leadership in a Global Context: New Directions in Research and Theory Development," *Journal of World Business* 47, no. 4 (2012): 479-482, https://doi.org/10.1016/j.jwb.2012.01.001.

[305] Schneider, "Why Good Management Ideas Fail."

[306] Northouse, *Leadership*.

[307] Trabucchi et al., "Sharing Economy: Seeing Through the Fog."

[308] Hofstede et al., *Cultures and Organizations: Software of the Mind*.

[309] Northouse, *Leadership*.

[310] Parker, "Practicing Conflict Resolution."

[311] Caligiuri, *Cultural Agility*.

[312] Dukes, "The Employee Experience."

[313] Antonios D. Kargas, and Dimitrios Varoutas, "On the Relation between Organizational Culture and Leadership: An Empirical Analysis," *Cogent Business & Management* 2, no. 1 (2015), https://doi.org/10.1080/23311975.2015.1055953.

skills drills focused on treating every individual as unique while treating all individuals with dignity and respect:[314] Said skills drills could be part of the leader's efforts for self-improvement as well as for subordinate and/or aspiring leaders[315] to engrain the approach deeper into the cultural DNA.[316] Critically, the leader must understand that culture change is a very difficult effort that typically takes much time; the leader must understand the current culture before attempting to change.[317]

SUMMARY

- Every individual should be recognized as unique while every person should be treated with dignity and respect.
- Every leader interaction is a negotiation and an opportunity to influence the member's commitment to the organization.
- These relational interactions are governed by complementary theories that address the nuances of in- and out-groups and that speak to the quality of relationships between leaders and followers.
- High quality relationships drive high quality performance.
- Culture captures the essence of these relationships and is more powerful than any management system or attempt to change if the change does not align to

---

314 Sosik and Jung, *Full Range Leadership Development*.
315 Ibid.
316 Schein, *Organizational Culture and Leadership*.
317 Ibid.

the culture; changing culture is a long-term effort that must not be undertaken lightly.
- Sense-giving and sensemaking are pervasive as interactions occur.

Chapter 5. Change Plus Seven (C+7)™

"Change is easy, but the people..."[318]

"Watch what people are cynical about, and you can often discover what they lack."[319]

"Change Management is 10 percent logical and 90 percent emotional."[320]

The chapter title is intended to alert the leader that before change is implemented the organizational members should be included to the maximum extent possible.[321] Change is inherently scary for most people within the organization regardless of level or position and, as such, people need time to participate, offer input, and to process the impact.[322] The following sections expand upon these ideas.

---

[318] Berenschot Quote from Joris Westhof, Wouter Ten Have, and Steven Ten Have, *The Social Psychology of Change Management* (O'Reilly Media, 2018).

[319] George S. Patton. "Watch What People Are Cynical About, and You Can Discover What They Lack," (n.d.), discov www.brainyquote.com/authors/george-s-patton-quotes.

[320] Lisa Hershman, "Harnessing the Power of Process," Hammer and Company Seminar Lecture, 2010. Note: This was part of the author's Hammer and Company journey to become recognized as a Process Master

[321] Cameron and Quinn, *Diagnosing and Changing Organizational Culture*.

[322] Simoes et al., "Improving Change Management."

CHARACTERISTICS OF CHANGE

Organizations face both planned and unplanned or, in more academic terms, continuous or discontinuous change: Change has also been described as evolutionary or revolutionary.[323] The continuous or evolutionary change can be invisible, e.g., slight deviations from the standard that aggregate over time, whereas the unplanned, discontinuous, or revolutionary change can be very disruptive, e.g., the pandemic's impact to society which completely disrupted the status quo.[324] Change is a constant yet many in leadership do not appear to accept or have awareness that change management is therefore a leader competency.[325] This may be the root cause of the high rate of failure for planned changed efforts[326] and the carnage that wreaks havoc within organizations as a result.[327]

THE CARNAGE OF CHANGE

The culture discussion in the prior chapter addressed the fact that change is typically rejected by the organizational culture[328] but did not go into detail. In this section and those that follow more specificity relative to change

---

[323] Warner W. Burke, *Organization Change: Theory and Practice* (Los Angeles, CA: Sage, 2018).

[324] Donald L. Anderson, *Organizational Development: The Process of Leading Organizational Change* (Los Angeles, CA: Sage, 2012).

[325] Paul Lawrence, "Leading Change – Insights into How Leaders Actually Approach the Challenge of Complexity," *Journal of Change Management* 15, no. 3 (2015): 231-52, https://doi.org/10.1080/14697017.2015.1021271.

[326] Victor Lipman, "Why Does Organizational Change Usually Fail? New Study Provides Simple Answer," Forbes, 2016, https://www.forbes.com/sites/victorlipman/2016/02/08/why-does-organizational-change-usually-fail-new-study-provides-simple-answer/#658440674bf8.

[327] Stanleigh, "Effecting Successful Change Management Initiatives."

[328] Lipman, "Why Does Organizational Change Usually Fail?"

will discussed. It is imperative that the leader, regardless of organizational level, is aware that most change related failure results from poor leader engagement with organizational members and this lack of engagement creates negativity, anxiety, fear, and cynicism.[329] In effect, leaders who do not engage the organizational members create highly charged, highly emotional environments as individuals attempt to process and understand how they will be impacted and what will be lost as a result of the changes.[330] Within this charged emotive environment organizational members will often transition through the various stages of grief with each individual progressing at differing rates until the changes are accepted or rejected.[331] This foundational understanding is why the author affirmatively states that change management is a key leader competency and must be attuned to the organization's - really the organizational culture's - readiness and receptivity for change.[332] If so attuned, the leader will be better prepared for the almost innate resistance that will occur as change is encountered.[333]

---

[329] Stanleigh, "Effecting Successful Change Management Initiatives."

[330] Will and Pies, "Sensemaking and Sensegiving."

[331] Stanleigh, "Effecting Successful Change Management Initiatives."

[332] Jeff Slattery, "Change Management," *Journal of Strategic Leadership* 4, no. 2 (2013): 1-5, https://www.regent.edu/acad/global/publications/jsl/vol4iss2/jslvol4iss2.pdf#page=59.

[333] Gary Hammel, *Leading the Revolution: How to Thrive in Turbulent Times by Making Innovation a Way of Life* (Boston, MA: Penguin Books, Ltd, 2002).

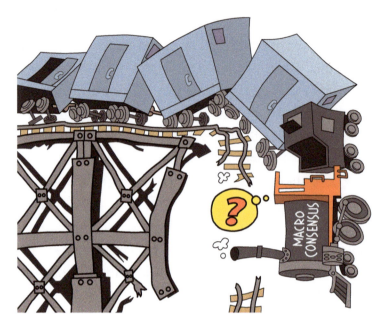

Figure 9: The Carnage of Change

THE ABCs OF RESISTANCE

Leaders will encounter resistance across three domains as change occurs. The domains are the affective, behavioral, and cognitive.[334] It is this tri-dimensional aspect of change resistance that links to the relational issues discussed earlier and the need for the leader to be skilled in Emotional Intelligence to better address resistance:[335] All aspects of Emotional Intelligence are in play during change resistance ergo its importance to the leader.[336] If

---

334 Philip J. Kitchen and Finbarr Daly, "Internal Communication during Change Management," *Corporate Communications: An International Journal* 7, no. 1 (2002): 46-53, https://doi.org/10.1108/13563280210416035.

335 Antonakis et al., "Does Leadership Need Emotional Intelligence?"

336 Molly Matthew and K. S. Gupta, "Transformational Leadership: Emotional Intelligence," *SCMS Journal of Indian Management* 12, no. 2 (2015): 75-89.

for nothing else, leaders need to be educated and trained in dealing with the ABCs of change resistance given the widespread occurrences of each.[337]

Affective

In the author's experience most leaders do not like to consider feelings and emotions as a workplace concern yet everyone emotes and emotions impact organizational performance.[338] Affective resistance may manifest as anxiety, stress, fear, anger, hurt, uncertainty, etc., as the members process the change and work through the grieving process.[339] Empathy, understanding, and sense-giving will be the leader's counterbalance to affective resistance if maintaining and increasing trust are important.[340]

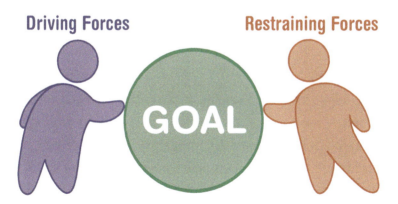

Figure 10: Resistance to Change

---

337 Kilkelly, "Creating Leaders for Successful Change Management."
338 Slattery, "Change Management."
339 Stanleigh, "Effecting Successful Change Management Initiatives."
340 Simoes et al., "Improving Change Management."

Behavioral

Behavioral resistance can range the gamut of questioning, delaying, to outright opposition and sabotage.[341] Conflict management skills are paramount as the leader anticipates and encounters behavioral resistance.[342] Importantly, members who deeply question the change may actually be receptive to and accepting of the change yet simply need more information and, potentially, more assurances from the leader that all will be well – questioning is part of Discovery Learning and the well-prepared leader will be ready to guide the conversation to the desired end.[343] Conversely, behavioral resistance may take on a more adversarial and counterproductive approach, especially from those in the out-group, hence the need for fine-tuned conflict management skills if the leader cannot assuage member concerns[344] via communications.[345]

Cognitive

Cognitive resistance relates to how the member thinks about, reasons, or perceives the pending change. Arguably this is a more fact-based rational approach to resistance that can be countered with the leader's facts via sense-giving;[346] however, the leader should not make this assumption given the interplay between and among the affective, behavioral, and cognitive forms of

---

341 Oster, "Listening to Luddites."
342 Singleton et al., "Workplace Conflict."
343 Lee, "Jesus Teaching Through Discovery."
344 Parker, "Practicing Conflict Resolution."
345 Düren, "Change Communication Can Be So Simple!"
346 Will and Pies, "Sensemaking and Sensegiving."

resistance.[347] The member could be in a state of cognitive dissonance wherein facts as perceived by the leader may not matter due to a highly emotive state.[348] The true change leader understands emotions must be addressed before the rational so planning for the cathartic effect is key.[349] The author learned early that people may simply need to BMC before accepting change and falling in to support the effort.

BMC: Bitch, Moan, and Complain

The author learned the formal BMC concept during his Theory of Constraints Jonah certification. This certification course used a multi-step buy-in process in which the author was taught to expect and to plan for people throughout the organization to BMC as part of the give and take of process change because people's comfort zones and turf would be disrupted. Further, the BMC exchanges could be the source of ideas and inputs not previously considered ergo a potentially rich source to be mined for added value.[350] It is during the BMC exchanges that the leader can entertain new ideas while concurrently communicating the rationale for the change via a narrative linked to the strategic outcome which is the heart of

---

347 Simoes et al., "Improving Change Management."

348 Emanuale Invernizzi, Stefani Romenti, and Michela Fumagalli, "Identity, Communication, and Change Management in Ferrari," *Corporate Communications: An International Journal* 17, no. 4 (2012): 483-497, https://doi.org/10.1108/13563281211274194.

349 Stephen Denning, *The secret Language of Leadership: How Leaders Inspire Action through Narrative* (San Franciso, CA: Jossey-Bass, 2007).

350 Michael Michalko, *Thinkertoys: A Handbook of Creative-Thinking Techniques* (Berkeley, CA: Ten Speed Press, 2006).

leadership communication and sense-giving.[351] From the author's perspective leaders should see member BMCing as a positive because of the opportunity to guide the exchanges and to influence the ABCs of resistance to a more positive end.[352] The author is not naïve however. There will be some who simply do not buy-in hence the earlier focus on conflict management skills.[353] Some will simply need an exit plan.[354] Regardless, engagement via deliberate communication is the leader's critical tool in leading change.[355]

COMMUNICATION

The academic literature is replete with books and articles that address the importance of communications relative to relationships and change management with the essence being leaders must be attuned to the organization's receptiveness to change.[356] This speaks yet again directly to the leaders' understanding of the population impacted by the change, or in Emotional Intelligence terms, being aware of the impact on others[357] to maximize the chances for successful change.[358]

---

[351] Sohad Murrar and Markus Brauer, "Overcoming Resistance to Change: Using Narratives to Create More Positive Intergroup Attitudes," *Association for Psychological Science* 28, no. 2 (2019): 164-169, https://doi.org/10.1177/0963721418818552.

[352] Will and Pies, "Sensemaking and Sensegiving."

[353] Katz and and Flynn, "Understanding Conflict Management Systems."

[354] Oster, "Listening to Luddites."

[355] Düren, "Change Communication Can Be So Simple!"

[356] Collyer, "Communication – The Route to Successful Change Management."

[357] Mathew and Gupta, "Transformational Leadership: Emotional Intelligence."

[358] Vasiliki Amarantou, Stergiani Kazakopoulou, and Dimitrios Chatzoudes, "Resistance to Change: An Empirical Investigation of Its Antecedents," *Journal of Organizational Change Management* 31, no. 2 (2018): 426-450, https://doi.org/10.1108/JOCM-05-2017-0196.

Many are not interested in the origins of words but in the instant case it is important to understand that communicate derives from a Latin word, *communicare*, which means to make something common or to share or to participate in the development of meaning.[359] At its essence communication was intended to be a dialogue that ensured mutual understanding and enhanced relationships.[360] If one takes this ancient meaning and applies it today one can easily see that in many cases resistance to change revolves around the quality of the leaders' communication efforts.[361] The ABCs of resistance discussed earlier, i.e., the affective, behavioral, and cognitive aspects of resistance,[362] may not be totally eliminated via a concerted communicative effort but very likely could be dampened and mitigated[363] if the actors have high-quality relationships that are based on trust and mutual respect[364] and the leaders ensure the members have the opportunity to participate in the change planning and implementation.[365]

The key learning point is that failure to plan for and to engage in active communications with those impacted by the proposed changes virtually guarantees the change effort will not be accepted and will fail[366] – communications become the media through which leaders inform,

---

359 Simoes et al., "Improving Change Management."
360 Ibid.
361 Ibid.
362 Ibid.
363 Slattery, "Change Management."
364 LeBlanc and Gonzalez-Roma, "LMX."
365 Slattery, "Change Management."
366 John Baldoni, *Great Communication Secrets of Great Leaders* (New York, NY: McGraw-Hill Education – Europe, 2003).

influence, assuage members concerns, gain and sustain trust, and ultimately gain buy-in.[367] Communications designed to target the various audiences within the affected population are an antecedent for successful change management.[368] Simply stated, communications combined with Emotional Intelligence are very powerful change management leverage points if understood as such.[369]

C+7™: SOCIALIZE THE CHANGE THEN IMPLEMENT

The C+7™ formula is simply a reminder that, before change is implemented, leaders have what the author considers an obligation to socialize the proposed changes. The seven is intended to reflect the time, e.g., a week, during which the proposed changes are communicated, actually shared with the affected population, and feedback is actively entertained. The socializing period may be weeks or months depending upon the complexity of the changes or, if time is a vital issue, the socializing period may be severely truncated. The key is to alert the affected population and provide time when practicable for the natural BMCing to occur and for the leader engagement that should result as the changes are processed.[370] It is during this socializing period that all organizational members, leaders and followers alike, engage in sensemaking and sense-giving.[371] This is value-added time

---
367 Denning, *The Secret Language of Leadership*.
368 Murrar and Brauer, "Overcoming Resistance to Change."
369 Meadows, *Leverage Points*.
370 Amarantou et al., "Resistance to Change."
371 Will and Pies, "Sensemaking and Sensegiving."

up front that positions the desired changes for a higher probability of long-term success.[372] It is not the author's intent that this C+7™ socializing period be indefinite and never ending given, at some point, leaders must be decisive.[373] The aforementioned leader, member, and situation triad should be used to gauge the socialization term.

There is much art in leadership.[374] This approach is more art than science and is dependent upon a multitude of variables that leaders must consider that have already been introduced, e.g., the organizational culture's receptivity and readiness for change[375] and the quality of relationships within the various dyads and groups.[376] The Emotional Intelligence aspect yet again arises as these variables overlay recognition and awareness by leaders of their respective members: Emotional Intelligence concerns are inevitably woven into the organizational fabric and must be part and parcel of every leadership action.[377]

Leaders must be attuned to the ABC's of resistance and be receptive to concerns.[378] Leaders who are candid and authentic will also not mask or hide the fact that they too are uncertain as to the ultimate impact of change given the ripple effects that may occur downstream.[379] This openness or humility in not knowing all

---

372 Murrar and Brauer, "Overcoming Resistance to Change."
373 United States, *Army Leadership: Competent, Confident, and Agile.*
374 Ibid.
375 Bryan J. Weiner, "A Theory of Organizational Readiness for Change," *Implementation Science* 4, no. 1 (2009), https://doi.org/10.1186/1748-5908-4-67.
376 Northouse, *Leadership.*
377 Gunkel et al., "Culture's Influence on Emotional Intelligence."
378 Simoes et al., "Improving Change Management."
379 Amelia Moslemi, "Essential Attributes and Behaviours of a Change Leader," Queens University IRC, 2011

the answers typically will alert the others in the affected population that everyone will be impacted and, if used in a positive manner, can be used to gain greater buy-in as leaders address the vision and the desired future state outcomes.[380] Succinctly, this allows leaders to address the transformative aspects of jointly becoming something new.[381] Mental agility is required as is a degree of humbleness since not everything is within the leaders control.[382]

SUMMARY

- To the practicable extent possible alert the affected population of proposed changes and provide time for sensemaking and sense-giving.
- Expect the ABCs of resistance, i.e., affective, behavioral, and cognitive, to occur during BMCing...this often provides a catharsis while providing a rich vein from which to mine new ideas, etc.
- Be authentic. Change will impact you, the leader, too and you truly do not know the final outcome.
- Socialize. Engage. But decide. Some may never get on the bus...and may need to exit the program.

---

380 Van Tongeren et al., "Humility."
381 Moslemi, "Essential Attributes and Behaviours of a Change Leader."
382 Van Tongeren et al., "Humility."

Section III. Process

Process is a ubiquitous word that most understand as the steps by which some task is accomplished. What is not always well understood is that *process* itself needs to be unmasked and understood at its essence before anyone can make improvements. Figure 11 depicts the fundamentals of every process, regardless of type of work, that must be understood before any process can be improved.[383] This figure will be discussed in more detail below. Further, the author's experience indicates there is much confusion about process given the number of techniques that can be applied in design and improvement, e.g., Total Quality Management (TQM), Theory of Constraints (TOC), Lean, Six Sigma, or Agile. Each of the approaches has been hyped via marketing and certification yet each has its benefits and its limitations based on intended usage and need. The key for leaders is to not be sold on any one process as the silver bullet for success but to use each as needed at the correct time and place. These approaches are simply tools in the leader's toolbox and are often much more effective when used in concert with other approaches. An effective but often derided technique to determine which approach is most appropriate is the Squiggly Line.

---

383 George et al., *Lean Six Sigma Pocket Toolbook.*

Supplier	Input	Process	Output	Customer
S	I	P	O	C
Paint Store	Purple Paint	Move Furniture Remove Pictures Fill Holes & Sand Dust Apply 1st Coat Apply 2rd Coat Clean-Up	Painted Room	Teenage Son
Admin @ Step 2	Title Search	Confirm Title Update Loan Doc Submit for Review Shedule Closing	Loan Application	Borrower

Figure 11: SIPOC – The Process of Process

The author was introduced to the Squiggly Line while studying process design and improvement. The Squiggly Line, though very simplistic, was utilized by senior leaders to help focus tool selection to calibrate process performance. Figure 12 reflects the Squiggly Line. Practitioners dedicated to one technique will push back on this which is okay. They should because this is their livelihood whereas, as a leader, you should make the decision how to proceed. You want to maintain flexibility in approach because of the difference between effectiveness and efficiency. You can be very effective with inefficiencies. You can also be very ineffective yet highly efficient. Many miss this point.[384] The author recommends you focus on effectiveness first given this is the source of cashflow[385]

---

384 Satya S. Chakravorty and Bryan Atwater, "How Theory of Constraints can be used to direct Preventive Maintenance," *Industrial Management* 36, no. 6 (1994): 10, http://eres.regent.edu:2048/login?url=https://search-proquest-com.ezproxy.regent.edu/docview/211615719?accountid=13479.

385 Kartik Modi, Harshal Lowalekar, and N. M. K. Bhatta, "Revolutionizing Supply Chain Management the Theory of Constraints Way: A Case Study," *International Journal of Production Research* 57, no. 11 (2018): 3335-3361, https://doi.org/10.1080/00207543.2018.1523579.

and customer satisfaction.[386] Think inventory turn metric and the need for speed to meet customer demand.[387] As you encounter the process constraint make the effectivity improvements you need then focus on efficiencies - this is counterintuitive to most but drives revenue.[388]

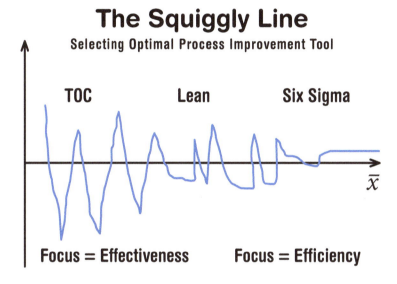

Figure 12: The Squiggly Line

There are two fundamental aspects of process that should be understood. First, regardless of type of work, every process will invariably develop a constraint or bottleneck.[389] This indicates that, at the heart of every

---

386 Ruchika Sharma, "12 Voice of the Customer Methodologies to Generate a Goldmine of Customer Feedback," Hubspot.com, 2019, https://blog.hubspot.com/service/voice-of-the-customer-methodologies.
387 Sharma, "12 Voice of the Customer Methodologies."
388 Chakravorty and Atwater, "How Theory of Constraints can be used."
389 Bryan J. Atwater and Satya S. Chakravorty, "Using the Theory of Constraints to Guide the Implementation of Quality Improvement Projects in Manufacturing Operations," *International Journal of Production Research* 33, no. 6 (1995): 1737-1760, https://doi.org/10.1080/00207549508930240.

organization, a constraint-based management approach should be implemented. Second, to mitigate the constraint, leaders should 'control the release' of inputs into the system so that inputs match what the constraint can produce.[390] There is both art and science to this which requires leaders to gain specific knowledge in this area. This is directly tied to cost, revenue, and earnings yet is often an enigma to those responsible for accomplishing work.[391]

The chapters below contain specific topics that drive organizational effectiveness. Each is a puzzle piece in the overall approach to process. If one is missing, then the process typically is not as effective as it could be. A key concern, a caveat, for leaders is to understand the point of diminishing returns,[392] i.e., the point where costs to continue improvement efforts exceed the gain or may even prove to have adverse impact.[393] This is a tough decision but one that should be a consideration because of the pressures many leaders face to engage in continuous improvement.[394] This is heresy to many singularly focused practitioners, especially those in Lean Six Sigma and Agile, but for the leader responsible and accountable for success this type hardcore determination

---

[390] Chakravorty and Atwater, "How Theory of Constraints can be used."

[391] Atwater and Chakravorty, "Using the Theory of Constraints."

[392] Amin Mahmoudi and Mohammad Reza Feylizadeh, "A Grey Mathematical Model for Crashing Projects by Considering Time, Cost, Quality, Risk and Law of Diminishing Returns," *Grey Systems: Theory and Application* 8, no. 3 (2018): 272-294, https://doi.org/10.1108/gs-12-2017-0042.

[393] Scott Mehall, "Purposeful Interpersonal Interaction and the Point of Diminishing Returns for Graduate Learners," *The Internet and Higher Education* 48, (January 2021), https://doi.org//10.1016/j.iheduc.2020.100774.

[394] Sobek and Smalley, *Understanding A3 Thinking*.

is a must.[395] At some point the leader must know whether continuous process improvement has become an ideology or if it leads to a product or service that the customer is willing to support; remember the SIPOC chart and keep in mind that the cost of improvements directly impact margin. A balance is required unless, like Elon Musk and Jeff Bezos, money is no longer a consideration. A 3-Sigma improvement may be all the customer wants. Conversely, if you opt to maintain the status quo you should minimally consider the power of S-Curve improvement to ensure status quo does not become stagnant and out-of-date.[396] The S-Curve technique will be discussed in more detail below.

SUMMARY

- Understand SIPOC. One member's output is likely the next member's input. If of poor quality then rework and member friction result. Both are costs that the leader should know.
- Balance improvement with return. Diminishing returns matter too.
- Do not be sold on efficiency over effectiveness.

---

395 United States, *Army Leadership: Competent, Confident, and Agile.*
396 Ghorbani, "The Philosophy behind S-Curves."

Chapter 6. Process: The Prerequisite to Effectiveness

"It is not necessary to change. Survival is not mandatory."[397]

"Results without process can't be replicated and process without results is worthless."[398]

It sounds self-evident that every organization has processes yet the author's experience is that many simply do not understand that fact or the implications of how processes work. One sees this across organizations as work throughput is stymied or backlogged.[399] The sections that follow will focus on key process considerations that the author has found universally applicable, i.e., pertinent to the leader regardless of type of organization, and that provide the leader better understanding of workflow.[400]

The author studied Total Quality Management during its heyday in the 1980s, ancient times for many, yet a critical time for Toyota and other Japanese manufacturers still heavily influenced by Deming as Japan continued

---
397 David A. Shore, *Launching and Leading Change Initiatives in Health Care Organizations* (San Francisco, CA: Jossey-Bass, 2014).
398 Anderson and Adams, *Mastering Leadership*.
399 Modi et al., "Revolutionizing Supply Chain Management."
400 George et al., *Lean Six Sigma Pocket Toolbook*.

rebuilding from World War II.[401] Deming taught the Japanese the techniques the US had implemented during the war to surge production. Deming, and others like him, taught the Japanese while their US counterparts reverted to pre-war techniques. In the 1970s and early 1980s we laughed at the Japanese quality whereas today we are still trying to emulate their quality and production techniques. Think about this clearly: We taught the Japanese Total Quality Management and the precursor techniques to Lean, i.e., Job Methods,[402] that were so successfully used in World War II. We forgot those approaches, and due to global quality issues, had to relearn them from the Japanese.[403] The author's sensei in Lean were trained in Japan even as the author was self-studying the precursor Job Methods approaches. These approaches to high-quality work, regardless of type of work, are immediately applicable. Think Toyota... the benchmark for most seeking effectiveness and efficiency.

THE PROCESS OF PROCESS: SIPOC

At the fundamental level every process is captured by the acronym SIPOC which stands for supplier, input, process, output, and customer.[404] Issues affecting workflow can be internal due to how work flows through the system or external because the internal work flow design

---

[401] S. M. Motzko, "Deming's 14 Points for Management: Variation, System Improvement," *Professional Safety* 34, no. 8 (1989).

[402] Tom Caldecott, "World War II Program Helps Manufacturers Stay Lean," AllBusiness.com, 2010, World War II Program Helps Manufacturers Stay Lean | AllBusiness.com.

[403] Sobek and Smalley, *Understanding A3 Thinking*.

[404] George et al., *Lean Six Sigma Pocket Toolbook*.

is not optimized to customer demand.[405] In the author's experience most organizations try to force work through the system by pushing work even as the process steps are not designed for such; invariably, work flows better when pulled through the system by customer demand.[406] Saying this is counterintuitive is an understatement for many given the cognitive resistance[407] to changing the approach. It takes effort for many to accept this due to the traditional approach to assigning work yet, for the mentally agile, seeing is believing once one experiences the change.[408]

For leaders it is imperative to understand that the SIPOC model is applicable at both the macro and micro levels, i.e., external and internal to the organization.[409] Within the organization Employee A's output may be Employee B's supplier and input while B is A's customer. This is best visualized via a process work breakdown structure that depicts each task and subtask within the macro process.[410] If Employee A's work is substandard then Employee B cannot perform successfully during the initial work effort. Employees C, D, and E are also impacted if the process contains other members. This is a classic example of a leader follower situation wherein

---

405 Modi et al., "Revolutionizing Supply Chain Management."
406 Ibid.
407 Sosik and Jung, *Full Range Leadership Development*.
408 Mohamad Alnajem, "Learning by Doing: An Undergraduate Lean A3 Project in a Kuwaiti Bank," *The TQM Journal* 33, no. 1 (2020): 71-94, https://doi.org/10.1108/tqm-01-2020-0010.
409 George et al., *Lean Six Sigma Pocket Toolbook*.
410 Kate Eby, "Getting Started with Work Breakdown Structures (WBS) | Smartsheet," Smartsheet.com, November 8, 2016, All About Work Breakdown Structures (WBS) | Smartsheet.

relationships are critical given the tangible and intangible costs involved with rework.[411]

Supplier	Input	Process	Output	Customer
S	**I**	**P**	**O**	**C**
Paint Store	Purple Paint	Move Furniture Remove Pictures Fill Holes & Sand Dust Apply 1st Coat Apply 2rd Coat Clean-Up	Painted Room	Teenage Son
Admin @ Step 2	Title Search	Confirm Title Update Loan Doc Submit for Review Shedule Closing	Loan Application	Borrower

Figure 13: SIPOC – The Process of Process

The SIPOC model is also important to understand because it provides the leader a systematic means to conduct analysis on where transformation and innovation may be targeted.[412] The author's experience indicates the process domain within the SIPOC model is typically the first area to be assessed given this is where the form, fit, or function of the input is modified to meet customer expectations.[413] The process area is where the future-oriented leader[414] will be seeking the moonshots or 100-fold increases in productivity that differentiates one organization from another.[415] Using the aforementioned squiggly line to assess the process domain's performance

---

411   Sosik and Jung, *Full Range Leadership Development*.
412   Modi et al., "Revolutionizing Supply Chain Management."
413   Sharma, "12 Voice of the Customer Methodologies."
414   Canton, *Future Smart*.
415   Diamandis and Kotler, *The Future Is Faster Than You Think*.

provides the leader a baseline from which to consider said moonshots.[416]

THE SQUIGGLY LINE

The Squiggly Line is a visual that is used to identify the most appropriate tool for process improvement. From left to right the best tool for improvement would be Theory of Constraints (TOC), then Lean, then Six Sigma. From the left the extreme variation indicates that the process is unstable and ineffective ergo the use of TOC to stabilize the process and to ensure effectiveness. In the center of the line the process is relatively stable and the use of Lean techniques to identify waste and to make efficiency improvements would be appropriate. At the far right of the line Six Sigma would be most appropriate given the process is highly stable and the opportunity to fine tune the process is present. One could add Agile to the above and its plot would be similar given the high degree of commonality between it and Lean.

---

416 Ibid.

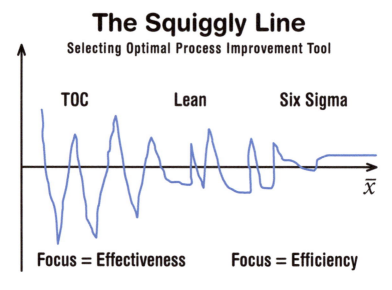

Figure 14: The Squiggly Line

It is at the middle and far right of the Squiggly Line that the leader will be pressured to enter into a continuous process improvement mode of operation and must exercise caution as the benefit of further resource application is considered; it is here that the point of diminishing returns discussion above rears its head as it may not be cost-effective to pursue the sixth sigma if the third or fourth sigma provides the customer a well-received product.[417] Again, this is heresy from the practitioner perspective so be aware. Of note, the Squiggly Line is applicable in every environment given the process improvement techniques above work in all environments if the leader has the mental agility to apply them. As the author's Lean sensei always emphasized *work is work*: The brain surgeon may argue this but he or she both

---

417 Modi et al., "Revolutionizing Supply Chain Management."

have a SIPOC just as the house painter and the bank loan officer.

As a side note, for hospitals, the patient may be the input, brain surgery the process, the patient the output, but the customer may actually be the surgeon and/or the insurer – the SIPOC can help simplify these type complexities.[418] For the leader responsible for work the key is to understand these complexities and the effectiveness of the organization's processes.

BLENDING PROCESS IMPROVEMENT APPROACHES

In the earlier discussion on change the author spoke to the unplanned, incremental change that naturally occurs within organizations.[419] This aspect of change often catches leaders by surprise when evaluating a process, i.e., the process one thinks exists may not exist due to incremental changes that were not recognized or codified in a governance document. This phenomenon alone speaks to the value of using the tools discussed in the Squiggly Line section. It also addresses the leader's mental agility and Emotional Intelligence as this situation is recognized, i.e., how does the leader react to this type finding.[420] Process variability becomes the key metric to monitor pending any planned moonshot.[421]

---

418 Steven M. Manson, "Simplifying Complexity: A Review of Complexity Theory," *Geoforum* 32, no. 3 (2001): 405-414, https://doi.org/10/1016/s0016-7185(00)00035-x.

419 Anderson, *Organizational Development*.

420 Mathew and Gupta, "Transformational Leadership: Emotional Intelligence."

421 George et al., *Lean Six Sigma Pocket Toolbook*.

Process variability is easily monitored via a Statistical Process Control (SPC) chart.[422] This is part of the Total Quality Management (TQM) approach proffered by Deming;[423] however, it can be used separately from the holistic implementation of a TQM program to give the leader near real-time visibility into process performance.[424] The critical take-away is that, even if the organizational culture does not or will not support a TQM implementation,[425] many of the tools within TQM can be used discretely; the SPC chart is one that every leader should have familiarity given it quickly depicts in real-time, assuming data are maintained, the process' performance.[426]

The SPC chart is applicable to TOC, Lean, and Six Sigma impacts as it is designed to depict process stability and process variability within three standard deviations of the process mean.[427] See Figure 15. If the process is highly unstable, ineffective, and the leader opts to implement TOC for improvement the SPC chart can depict this situation and visually highlight TOC's impact as constrained resources and bottlenecks are attacked and eliminated.[428] Similarly, as the leader has stabilized the process and turns to making it more efficient via a Lean

---

422 Russell Hills, "Statistical Process Control Basic Control Charts." YouTube, 2015, https://www.youtube.com/watch?v=WdqSm0DiYtY.
423 Motzko, "Deming's 14 Points for Management."
424 Juan Antonio Gimenez-Espin, Daniel Jimenez-Jimenez, and Micaela Martinez-Costa, "Organizational Culture for Total Quality Management," *Total Quality Management and Business Excellence* 24, no. 5-6 (2013): 678-692, https://doi.org/10.1080/14783363.21012.707409.
425 Gimenez-Espin et al., "Organizational Culture for Total Quality Management."
426 George et al., *Lean Six Sigma Pocket Toolbook*.
427 George et al., *Lean Six Sigma Pocket Toolbook*.
428 Modi et al., "Revolutionizing Supply Chain Management."

approach the SPC will capture the impacts visually as the data begin to cluster more proximate to the mean.[429] And finally, if the leader pursues a Six Sigma approach the SPC chart will depict performance virtually aligning to the mean.[430]

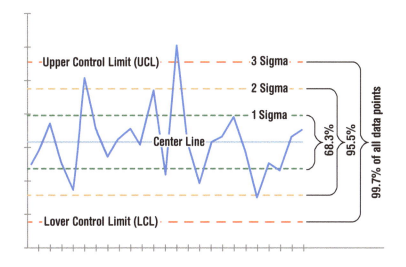

Figure 15: Statistical Process Control Chart

If the leader uses the SPC chart as part of a visual management approach then the organizational members and stakeholders will be able to see the results at any time.[431] This is a powerful incentive for amplifying performance in the author's experience. From this simple chart everyone will be able to determine if the process is 'in control' or 'out of control'[432] and, if the culture supports employee empowerment, the members will be

---

429 George et al., *Lean Six Sigma Pocket Toolbook.*
430 Ibid.
431 Ibid.
432 Ibid.

automatically reacting to out of control situations without need for a leader reaction.[433] For the leaders who practice Gemba walks, or deliberate visits to the places where work is performed to observe the work being performed,[434] this will be one of the first metrics viewed given its real-time process performance depiction.

Note there are even more powerful nuances related to SPC charts,[435] but they exceed the parameters of this book. Leaders would do well to take the time to understand these. If used, the leader can simply monitor the process for cruise control like performance until such time as a planned process improvement is scheduled, e.g., via an S-Curve event.[436] This will be addressed in more detail in a subsequent chapter. And, as a reminder, embedded in this process discussion are the critical links to culture and member relationships; if the culture is not primed for this approach the leader will experience failure.[437]

CONTROLLED RELEASE OF WORK

In the Acknowledgement section of this book the author recognized Dr. Satya Chakravorty, now deceased. He and the author had numerous conversations relative to this topic given his Operational Management and TOC expertise during their work together in an Air Force manufacture, repair, and overhaul depot, known as an Air Logistics Complex (ALC). From their conversations the

---

433 Modi et al., "Revolutionizing Supply Chain Management."
434 Alnajem, "Learning by Doing."
435 Hills, "Statistical Process Control Basic Control Charts."
436 Ghorbani, "The Philosophy Behind S-Curves."
437 Gimenez-Espin et al., "Organizational Culture For Total Quality Management."

author learned the importance of this concept as it relates to the differences between a push and pull workflow.[438] Simply stated, if work is released into a work process in an uncontrolled manner the process will jam as the process constraints are encountered.[439] This is the classical push system that most leaders use routinely: To be most effective, i.e., most profitable, work should be released in a controlled manner as it is pulled into the process based on customer demand.[440]

During their time at the ALC Dr. Chakravorty and the author worked both industrial and administrative constraints, e.g., the F-15 production line and a large backlog of disciplinary and grievance workload in the Human Resources (HR) office. In both instances it was determined that the supervisors were simply pushing work into the work process without consideration of the impact to the system or to the timely output of work. Both work units were behind in schedule and cost. After taking time to enhance leader understanding of process management both work units realigned work release to the constraints within the system and very quickly caught up then stabilized output. Subsequent to their departure both work units returned to the status quo ante and soon reverted to untimely work and lost revenue.[441] Neither culture was receptive to the changes even though the results were

---

[438] Modi et al., "Revolutionizing Supply Chain Management."
[439] Atwater and Chakravorty, "Using the Theory of Constraints."
[440] Modi et al., "Revolutionizing Supply Chain Management."
[441] Ibid.

very positive.[442] The organization's culture must be receptive to change even in the technical aspects of process.[443]

THE INTERSECTION OF CULTURE AND PROCESS

Culture is responsible for over two thirds of process change efforts failing.[444] The issue becomes one of receptivity and readiness for change as discussed earlier,[445] e.g., the culture may not be structurally matched to the change effort.[446] Typically, TOC, Lean, Six Sigma, and Agile seek to empower the process members to monitor and effect improvements with little to no direct supervision once guidance and change parameters are in place. Cultures that focus on the customer, are flexible, seek training and development, and allow a high degree of employee empowerment do much better in the process improvement arena than other cultural types, e.g., control-oriented cultures that seek a high degree of stability[447] and use a 'wash, rinse, repeat' approach to work performance. The latter is simply unsuited for the dynamics of sustainable process improvement without experiencing a major shift in orientation to be successful via employee empowerment.[448]

The leader must be attuned to the nuances of the existing culture well before attempting to alter existing

---

442 Ibid.
443 Gimenez-Espin et al., "Organizational Culture for Total Quality Management."
444 Ibid.
445 Weiner, "A Theory of Organizational Readiness For Change."
446 Gimenez-Espin et al., "Organizational Culture for Total Quality Management."
447 Cameron and Quinn, *Diagnosing and Changing Organizational Culture*.
448 Ibid.

processes in a significant manner. This is the point made in an earlier chapter that organizational members will often attempt to wait out a new senior leader or commander and only make superficial change efforts.

WIP – WORK IN PROGRESS

The controlled release of work segues directly into Little's Law which is a queuing theory consideration, i.e., an approach to determine the efficiency of any queuing system, e.g., a coffee shop, a supermarket check-out, or the number of planes in a repair line.[449] Little's Law is important to leaders, especially when coupled with the controlled release of work technique, because it provides visibility into how much work in progress (WIP)[450] should be in the system at any one time.[451] If your organization has any type sequential or queuing process, i.e., a system where work enters and leaves, then Little's Law is key to understanding your current and any prospective systems.[452] Little's Law fits neatly into the SIPOC process discussed earlier as it applies to the P part of the acronym; however, it only concerns the item as a whole going through the system; it does not pertain to the sub-steps in play unless it is specifically applied within the sub-step. This is a critical nuance that adds to its power.[453]

---

449 "Little's Law – Overview, Formula and Practical Example," Corporate Finance Institute, 2019, https://corporatefinanceinstitute.com/resources/knowledge/other/littles-law/.

450 Ben Mulholland, "Little's Law: How to Analyze Your Processes (with Stealth Bombers)," Process Street, November 20, 2017, https://www.process.st/littles-law/.

451 "Little's Law - Overview."

452 Mulholland, "Little's Law."

453 Ibid.

Little's Law is vital to TOC, Lean, and Agile approaches to process improvement as it speaks to the work that exits the system.[454] As a caveat Little's Law is only applicable in a stable system which links back to the Squiggly Line and the SPC tool.[455]

In the traditional release of work approach supervisors divvy work out to employees based on whatever protocol exists for assignments and employees invariably have multiple items of work in progress at any one time. In administrative transactional offices for example employees may be assigned dozens of files to work at any one time. This approach to WIP typically results in the employee repeatedly stopping and starting work on individual WIP items. This is usually viewed as multitasking[456] which is a very common requirement in job announcements. To those not versed in process this approach is normal, comfortable, and not recognized as a contributor to higher costs, missed schedules, and unnecessary conflict within the organization and typically with the customer. To the trained eye the problem with this approach is each start-stop cycle[457] is in effect a set-up tear-down cycle similar to a machine set up for custom jobs wherein every job requires a set-up tear-down before the next job can begin. If the machinist is constantly given changed assignments multiple unfinished items become inventory that then must be managed. The employee must

---

454 Ibid.
455 "Little's Law – Overview."
456 Nancy K. Napier, "The Myth of Multitasking: Think You can Multitask Well? Think Again," Psychology Today, May 12, 2014, https://www.psychologytoday.com/us/blog/creativity-without-borders/201405/the-myth-of-multitasking.
457 Napier, "The Myth of Multitasking."

consciously shift from one WIP item to the next, recall what was done and where the work was left in progress, what needs to be done, what resources are required, etc., before beginning to work the WIP item. Regardless, if machinist or transactional employee all this mental recall and physical re-set equates to lost production time which can easily be monetized or dollarized as a tangible cost to the organization, and if tracked, to the individual's level of performance.[458] Typically, however, this lost time, lost production, and lost revenue remain unseen. This phenomenon is overcome by a focus on completing one WIP item before another is started which is easily done via setting WIP limits[459] or implementing one-piece flow where an item must be finished (output) before another can be started (input).[460]

Multitasking is typically a negative to the organization even though the Human Resource department invariably has this as a required work competency. Multitasking increases stress and errors as well as costing time because humans do not have the capacity to do two or more tasks simultaneously – people can only switch tasks sequentially.[461] A leader should seek to avoid multitasking to the extent possible due to the hidden costs involved and to the much lower level of work that is produced at any one time.[462] Via the controlled release of work into the system and an understanding of how work flows through a system leaders can obviate this hidden cost and have

---
458 Ibid.
459 Mulholland, "Little's Law."
460 George et al., *Lean Six Sigma Pocket Toolbook*.
461 Napier, "The Myth of Multitasking."
462 Ibid.

more success in the quality of work performed as well as enhanced schedule and cost performance.

SUMMARY

- Leadership becomes vital at the convergence of People and Process.
- Leaders should know SIPOC, the process of process, to better see leverage points for transformation and innovation.
- The Statistical Process Control chart enhances leader understanding of process performance.
- The controlled release of work and using pull systems are key to highly effective workflows, i.e., profitability.
- Culture must be understood before process changes are implemented else failure is highly probable.
- WIP is a key variable to know and it should be linked to customer demand.
- Avoid multi-tasking unless money and time are of no concern.

Chapter 7. Velocity

"Theory of Constraints (TOC): A Thinking Process that enables people to invent simple solutions to complex problems."[463]

The author is fundamentally convinced that TOC should be the foundational design to workflow regardless of organization type given its focus on throughput of the product or service that generates revenue: TOC is focused on organizational effectiveness which should be at the forefront of every leader's thinking.[464] Lean and Lean Six Sigma are focused on efficiency which is a cost concern but neither focuses *per se* on revenue generation.[465] Agile assumes work backlog[466] which TOC seeks to preclude or eliminate via constraint management because backlog drives inventory, a major operating

---

463 Kate Eby, "Everything You Need to know about Theory of Constraints | Smartsheet," Smartsheet.com, July 24, 2017, Ultimate Guide to Theory of Constraints | Smartsheet.

464 Modi et al., "Revolutionizing Supply Chain Management."

465 Kate Eby, "Everything You Need to know about Lean Six Sigma | Smartsheet," Smartsheet.com, June 16, 2017, https://www.smartsheet.com/all-about-lean-six-sigma.

466 Kate Eby, "Everything You Need to know about Agile Project Management | Smartsheet," Smartsheet.com, September 23, 2016, Agile One-Stop Project Management Resource | Smartsheet.

expense.[467] Many will disagree. Just understand there is a critical distinction between effectiveness and efficiency that TOC addresses – the two are not interchangeable.[468] From the author's perspective efficiency is not the primary focus ergo TOC is the foundational process design. Only after the process is flowing is Lean Six Sigma or Agile applied to ensure velocity of work going through the system to maximize revenue generation or service provision.[469] And, as a forewarning, it is important to understand constraints can also include policies, measurements, and behaviors in addition to workflow.[470] Be open to all these potential concerns.

TOC PHILOSOPHY

Leaders who apply TOC benefit from the approach's perspective that every system, regardless of complexity, has one key constraint that impacts workflow.[471] If this constraint is identified and resolved the system will generate the next constraint which can then be identified and resolved *ad infinitum*.[472] See Figure 16. This perspective simplifies complexity[473] and allows the leader to focus on the key limitation to effectiveness.[474] Critically, every

---

467 Kettering Global, "5 Steps to Understanding and Applying the Theory of Constraints," Kettering Global, July 25, 2016, https://online.kettering.edu/news/2016/07/25/5/-steps-understanding-and-applying-theory-of-constraints.
468 Kettering Global, "Theory of Constraints."
469 Ibid.
470 Ibid.
471 Ibid.
472 Atwater and Chakravorty, "Using the Theory of Constraints."
473 Brian Duignan, "Occam's Razor | Origin, Examples, & Facts," Encyclopedia Britannica, 2018, https://www.britannica.com/topic/Occams-razor.
474 Kettering Global, "Theory of Constraints."

system will stall if the work release and the workflow are not controlled and timed to the primary constraint - the system simply cannot produce faster than the primary constraint and any effort to force work through the system simply generates unnecessary partial work inventories and increases costs.[475] Of note, a key takeaway is that TOC literally exposes new capacity without the requirement for new machinery or manpower if applied correctly.[476] Critically, TOC looks at the system via a holistic perspective.[477] This is also reflected in the global approach to accounting in a TOC environment.

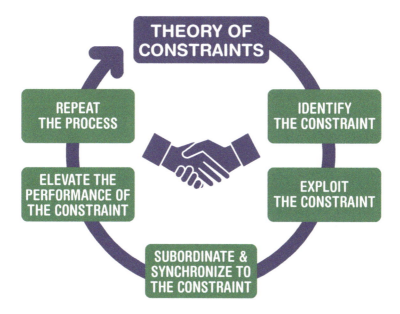

Figure 16: TOC Process Steps

---

475 Atwater and Chakravorty, "Using the Theory of Constraints."
476 Eby, "Theory of Constraints."
477 Ibid.

ACCOUNTING IN A TOC ENVIRONMENT

The TOC approach to accounting requires a paradigm shift for many in that it focuses on three global items, i.e., throughput (sales minus cost of raw material), inventory (money tied up within the company), and operating expense (money spent converting raw materials and inventory into throughput) in lieu of the traditional approach that subdivides the budget into numerous categories that often distorts the bottom line.[478] Adoption of Throughput Accounting significantly changes the perspective as cost is not the only consideration and a systemic approach versus activity-based accounting is the norm.[479] Maximizing throughput is the goal hence the desire for velocity. The financial types not versed in this approach often experience cognitive dissonance due to the focus on efficiency.

THE TOC PROCESS

There are innumerable articles on the application of TOC with many discussing the drum, buffer, rope (DBR) concept in its various forms.[480] The author is versed in the DBR approaches and has used them extensively because they work. Overall, the TOC process is so good that it has proliferated to growing economies like India's because of the focus on effectiveness, i.e., throughput of products or services that generate revenue. In India TOC is seen as more appropriate than the typical contemporary advisory focus on efficiency by major western consulting

---
478 Kettering Global, "Theory of Constraints."
479 Ibid.
480 Chakravorty and Atwater, "How Theory of Constraints can be used."

firms because the small to medium sized family-owned businesses are leery of the westernized approach to consulting; these small to medium sized businesses want the consultant to have skin in the game with compensation at least partly based on results.[481]

With this cultural mindset TOC has found a solid footing in India as TOC focuses on one constraint at a time versus attempting broader interventions.[482] This focus helps leverage the critical point in time and space that generates the most results to drive revenue for the client and the consultant: "If there is an enormous rock in your path, the easiest and simplest way to remove it is by using a crowbar or metal rod to pry it out of the way. But for the best results the rod had to be wedged against the rock at one particular point (the fulcrum) which can give you maximum leverage".[483] In these two sentences the power of TOC's holistic perspective on maximizing throughput to generate revenue is highlighted.[484] Examples of success in India that are immediately relatable to any organization world-wide include:[485]

- 20-50% increase in Net Sales
- 20-40% reduction in Inventory
- 10-30% reduction in Bills Receivables
- Shift from less than 10% on-time delivery to 90%

---

481 A. Bhattacharyya, "Conventional Management Approach is a Misfit Today, Says Vector Consulting Director," Business Today, 2016, Conventional management approach is a misfit today, says Vector Consulting Director (businesstoday.in).
482 Chakravorty and Atwater, "How Theory of Constraints can be used."
483 Bhattacharyya, "Conventional Management Approach is a Misfit Today."
484 Kettering Global, "Theory of Constraints."
485 TOC Institute, "TOC in India," TOC Institute, 2020, TOC in India - Theory of Constraints Institute (tocinstitute.org).

- 20-40% faster implementation of large projects

The TOC process is a logic-based approach to workflow that offers high value to the user. Discussion of DBR's many forms is critical for deeper understanding of TOC's value but likely part of the author's next effort. For the current reader the two key concepts for deeper understanding are the controlled release of work into the system and slack.

Controlled Release of Work

In the discussion above the author has introduced the controlled release of work at a high level. Within the TOC process work release is controlled via the use of buffers or holding areas for pending work.[486] Buffers can be positioned in front of every step in the work breakdown structure[487] to ensure work is pulled into the work process as opposed to being pushed into it.[488] This pull technique ensures work is released only when the work process can actually execute the required process steps to complete the work.[489] This precludes the accumulation of partial work that push systems generate, i.e., work that must be set aside and managed as inventory because the next step in the process is not able to complete the work.[490]

If you recall the SIPOC discussion earlier this speaks to one process step's output being the next process

---

[486] Atwater and Chakravorty, "Using the Theory of Constraints."
[487] Eby, "Work Breakdown Structures."
[488] George et al., *Lean Six Sigma Pocket Toolbook*.
[489] Chakravorty and Atwater, "How Theory of Constraints can be used."
[490] Ibid.

step's input;[491] if the downstream process step cannot produce the input it must be set aside and managed as an unnecessary cost to the organization.[492] Of specific concern partially completed work can accumulate in front of each work step which means there literally are multiple inventories with each having different sets of partially completed work and different management requirements to maintain them; if not obviated this can become an invisible major operating expense.[493] The controlled release of work infers employees at non-constrained process steps may be idle at times to avoid producing partial work. WARNING: This drives control-oriented leaders and HR types crazy and it often creates fear among members accustomed to an efficiency focus that requires constant activity.

The buffer management and employee idleness approach is counterintuitive if not alien to many given the typical leader and HR perspectives that every employee must always be working to maximize efficiency.[494] From the TOC perspective it may be more cost-wise, more cost effective if employees are idle instead of producing partial work; employee inefficiency may be perfectly acceptable if creating unnecessary inventory or backlogged work can be avoided.[495] This is a leader paradigm shift as seeing[496] employees idle generates anxiety if the bigger picture of

---

491 George et al., *Lean Six Sigma Pocket Toolbook*.
492 Kettering Global, "Theory of Constraints."
493 Kettering Global, "Theory of Constraints."
494 Ibid.
495 Ibid.
496 Trabucchi et al., "Sharing Economy: Seeing through the Fog."

effectiveness is not only understood but accepted.[497] If one views the process flow from the holistic perspective the old adage 'a penny wise, a pound foolish' makes sense. Be careful of Lean/Lean Six Sigma suboptimization at the cost of overall effectiveness.

Slack

The traditional approach to project management uses critical path methodologies with each step in the process containing time estimates.[498] It is not unusual for the project team to inflate time per inchstone or milestone to build safety into the project. This is referred to as float or slack and is often very costly as it provides a false sense of time within the project and often ends up wasted as the project invariably is late.[499] Within a TOC application critical path is replaced with critical chain project management which does not use inchstones or milestones to track completion.[500] Instead, the leader controls the project time and the project team is simply charged to go as fast as possible within safety, quality, and resource constraints.[501] The author's immediate rule of thumb whenever presented with a time estimate is to immediately reduce it by 50, if not 75 percent, as experience with slack or float indicates the work can be done within the remaining time allocated. If the leader

---

497 Kettering Global, "Theory of Constraints."
498 Peter Landau, "A Quick Guide to Float (or Slack) in Project Management," ProjectManager.com, June 24, 2020, https://www.projectmanager.com/blog/float-in-project-management.
499 Villanova University, "What is Critical Chain Project Management?" 2021, What is Critical Chain Project Management? (villanovau.com).
500 Villanova University, "Critical Chain Project Management."
501 Ibid.

understands critical chain and the DBR approach to work then speed with quality becomes the norm.[502] Any concerns with quality can be further reduced at the appropriate time by implementing Lean's poka yoke or error proofing techniques.[503]

Note this becomes a trust issue with organizational members unless the leader communicates effectively and is very conscientious in relationship management.[504] Shifting to a TOC and critical chain approach is, again, counterintuitive as most are not versed in constraint identification and subordination of all other efforts to the constraint or to the elimination of the historical slack within project work.[505] This is a pure change management concern with all its perturbations.[506]

VELOCITY

The TOC approach to workflow and product or service throughput is all about identifying and eliminating constraints to ensure smooth throughput of whatever product or service is in play.[507] Speed of work is typical; however, velocity is the true goal as it maximizes revenue potential.[508] To gain velocity you must integrate Lean, Lean Six Sigma, and potentially Agile techniques to the TOC

---

502 Ibid.
503 George et al., *Lean Six Sigma Pocket Toolbook.*
504 Sin et al., "Understanding Why They Don't See Eye to Eye."
505 Villanova University, "Critical Chain Project Management."
506 Steven Ten Have, John Risman, Wouter Ten Have, and Joris Westhof, *The Social Psychology of Change Management* (Routledge, 2018).
507 Modi et al., "Revolutionizing Supply Chain Management."
508 Dee Jacob, Suzan Bergland, and Jeff Cox, *Velocity: Combining Lean, Six Sigma and the Theory of Constraints to Achieve Breakthrough Performance* (New York, NY: Free Press, 2010).

workflow with the most value added if these techniques are targeted to the constraint area as this may increase profit.[509] It is a waste to apply Lean or Lean Six Sigma to non-constraint areas; no time or other resource applications to improve these areas are value-added.[510] Again, a heretical perspective that the leader must take to avoid unnecessary waste of time, energy, and resources. This is Lean in reverse from the leader perspective instead of the practitioner's perspective.

Specific to Lean and Lean Six Sigma the identification of waste and process variability provides opportunities to fine tune the workflow.[511] The Squiggly Line discussed earlier speaks to this indirectly as TOC, Lean, and Lean Six Sigma opportunities will overlap as the Squiggly Line tightens.[512]

Lean/Lean Six Sigma

Lean is focused on the identification and elimination of waste. Classical Lean identifies seven wastes which are transportation, inventory, motion, waiting, over processing, overproduction, and defects.[513] The Air Force considered misused or not used intellect to be an additional source of organizational waste;[514] this speaks indirectly

---

509 Jacob et al., *Velocity*.
510 University of Tennessee, *AFSO21: Air Force Smart Ops for the 21st Century* (The University of Tennessee Center for Executive Education, 2009).
511 Jacob et al., *Velocity*.
512 Ibid.
513 Eby, "Lean Six Sigma."
514 University of Tennessee, *AFSO21: Air Force Smart Ops for the 21st Century*.

to employee empowerment and input versus micromanagement, the "shut up and color" syndrome.[515]

One immediately sees how Lean can be used to enhance the TOC workflow by focusing on partial work inventory elimination. Application of Lean at the constraint makes sense whereas applying Lean to process steps before or after the constraint likely do not until the constraint shifts. Thus, applying Lean in the most effective way links its application to the constraint management process. Lean and Lean Six Sigma consultants will try to sell the organization on doing Lean via an infinite or '1 over n' approach which means every part of the organization needs to be doing Lean events. From a global operating expense perspective this may not be cost effective. Be skeptical of this recommendation. Target Lean to the constraint. When the constraint shifts retarget the Lean effort.

Six Sigma addresses variation in the process. This is important as variation creates turbulence which decreases speed and negates velocity. Process variation needs to be identified and resolved ergo the use of the aforementioned SPC chart to monitor process performance.[516] The SPC chart is a powerful tool if the process data are accurately maintained; however, as with the application of Lean be skeptical relative to attaining true six sigma – there is value to do so in many cases but less so in others as the point of diminishing returns is a

---

[515] Philip M. Podsakoff, Scott B. McKenzie, Robert H. Moorman, and Richard Fetter, "Transformational Leader Behaviors and Their Effects on Followers' Trust in Leader, Satisfaction, and Organizational Citizenship Behaviors," *Leadership Quarterly* 1, no. 2 (1990): 107-142, https://doi.org/10.1016/1048-9843(90)90009-7.

[516] George et al., *Lean Six Sigma Pocket Toolbook*.

key consideration.[517] Again, this is heresy to practitioners so understand the pressure from consultants to proceed. Also be very attuned to the Voice of the Customer – if the customer is unwilling to pay for these improvements there is no value added.[518]

The learning point is that the savvy application of Lean and Lean Six Sigma approaches to a TOC application leverages the strengths of each technique while ensuring a focus on effectiveness first, i.e., revenue generation, then amplifies process performance via fine tuning its efficiency to continue to add value via elimination of waste and/or to reduce the costs of variability.[519] There is both art and science involved as any improvement beyond the point of diminishing return creates negativity within the human element and within the financials.[520]

Daily Math

Every organization has requirements that must be accomplished that are in addition to its core functions, e.g., reports, budget preparation, annual employee ratings, etc. These requirements must be factored into the organization's work even if they do not support additional manpower or full-time equivalents. The output formula remains the same, i.e., quantity divided by time.[521] To produce this book the author divided the expected word count by the number of days before the draft was to be delivered to derive a daily writing requirement quota to

---

517 Mahmoudi et al., "A Grey Mathematical Model for Crashing Projects."
518 Sharma, "12 Voice of the Customer Methodologies."
519 Jacob et al., *Velocity*.
520 Mahmoudi et al., "A Grey Mathematical Model for Crashing Projects."
521 George et al., *Lean Six Sigma Pocket Toolbook*.

complete the task. Constancy of purpose,[522] discipline, and resilience are required if velocity is to be attained. Some days simply grinding through the requirement is a necessity.

A literal count of requirements is very helpful to ensure the leader is aware of all every single performance expectation. As an example, Dr. Chakravorty and the author guided the Air Force depot's HR office in determining daily work output requirements by having the leadership team categorize and account for all requirements. This number was divided by twelve to determine monthly requirements, then by twenty to determine daily requirements, then by eight to determine hourly requirements. That number was then divided by the number of office employees to determine the daily production requirement per employee. This approach was eye opening to the leadership team even as its application proved very effective – throughput from the office increased dramatically.[523]

The formula, quantity divided by time divided by employees, addresses the macro requirement as it is a gross application. Within the Lean/Lean Six Sigma environment this gross calculation is finessed to reflect both total and available times which become important as the function's core work is performed within the available time subset, and depending upon the complexity of the work process, may be parsed to expected production per second.[524] It is not unusual for work to be tracked in

[522] University of Tennessee, *AFSO21: Air Force Smart Ops for the 21st Century*.
[523] Eby, "Theory of Constraints."
[524] George et al., Lean Six Sigma Pocket Toolbook.

this manner; however, this approach is terrifying to those not reared in an industrial or manufacturing environment – white collar or those engaged in knowledge work typically do not think this way…but the organizational leader should due to the focus on effectiveness and revenue generation.[525] Seconds count if time is money.

As awareness, please note this section is intentionally titled – the fact that the function will not always be staffed or manned at 100 percent does not relieve the leader from the daily production requirement. Organizational members must be coached and mentored that organizational success is on the line.[526] This defaults to the trust, mutual respect, and mutual obligation that exists between leader and members and speaks to the leader's ability to vision cast expectations.[527] Velocity is dependent upon the leader knowing the daily math. If not executed work backlogs which only compounds the daily math expectations. Unless the leader's leader makes an exception to his or her performance expectations the leader must perform.

Agile

The author is aware that Agile is a very popular process approach that has evolved well beyond its software development roots.[528] Agile has its place but given its similarity

---

[525] Villanova University, "Critical Chain Project Management."
[526] Sosik and Jung, *Full Range Leadership Development*.
[527] Helen Campbell Pickford and Genevieve Joy, "Organizational Citizenship Behaviours: Definitions and Dimensions," SSRN Electronic Journal, 2016, https://doi.org/10.2139/ssrn.2893021.
[528] Eby, "Agile Project Management."

to Lean and its acceptance of backlog[529] the author does not recommend it as the basis for velocity. If Agile is in use the author would recommend that the Kanban technique within Agile be used because it addresses the need to limit WIP and, like TOC, it does not impose inchstone or milestone time limits.[530] Kanban pulls work from the backlog based on its WIP calculations to attempt to gain a smooth workflow.[531] This is similar to TOC in that work is stored in a buffer before its controlled release into the process; however, backlog results from the Agile team not being able to meet Scrum timelines.[532] There is a not so subtle difference given Scrum, like most non-TOC project management efforts, fails often[533] otherwise the Scrum teams would not be so postured.[534] The author perceives Agile to be a very well marketed technique.

SUMMARY

- Every system has constraints and constraints shift. The TOC steps are ad *infinitum* as long as that process exists or until the point of diminishing returns is reached.
- Velocity results from the adroit blending of process tools at the constraint.
- Daily Math is critical to velocity and backlog avoidance. Daily Math requires proactive change management to gain member buy-in to the approach.

---
529 Ibid.
530 Ibid.
531 Ibid.
532 Ibid.
533 Villanova University, "Critical Chain Project Management."
534 Eby, "Agile Project Management."

Chapter 8. Raising the Bar

"Daniel 6:3 - Then this Daniel began distinguishing himself among the commissioners and satraps because he possessed an extraordinary spirit, and the king planned to appoint him over the entire kingdom".[535]

Welcome to leadership. That was one of the author's favorite lines to new supervisors or managers when they were suddenly faced with a tasking that was clearly outside their portfolio, budget, and manpower and was usually accompanied by an insanely short suspense to execute. The tasking invariably led to efforts to reorganize work to free up capability and capacity. It was during these type events that the author learned the necessity to see[536] work differently to identify and capture hidden capacity and capability within existing resources.[537]

The remainder of this chapter touches on different tools and techniques that provide the leader greater visibility

---

535 *New American Standard Bible* (Lockman Foundation,1995), https://bible.knowing-jesus.com.

536 Theodore Kinni, "Seeing, Doing, and Imagining," Strategy+Business, 2021, https://www.strategy-business.com/blog/Seeing-doing-and-imagining?.

537 Alnajem, "Learning by Doing."

and leverage into the organization's performance.[538] The tools and techniques are typically technical or hard skill in nature;[539] however, do not forget the earlier discussion on the leader's role in preparing organizational members for these type requirements in advance via vision casting and narrative.[540] The organizational citizenship behaviors required to support raising the bar emanate from the trust and loyalty of the members to the leader;[541] if the leader has not laid the groundwork earlier for these type sudden process shifts the likelihood of success is small. People and process must be worked together.[542]

SEEING

Learning to see differently postures the leader to better understand the organizational environment in all its forms and to better understand how to be more effective. Learning to see clears the fog of daily pressures and politics.[543] In the author's experience leaders are not well versed in seeing as defined here, i.e., the ability to quickly assess the status of a workflow or process performance, especially in administrative or transactional environments not traditionally associated with operations or industrial management. In many instances, leaders are promoted from the toolbox or the cubicle without benefit

---

538 Luciana Teixeira Lot, Alice Sarantopoulos, Li Li Min, Simone Reges Perales, Ilka de Fatima Santana Ferreira Boin, and Elaine Cristina de Ataide, "Using Lean Tools to Reduce Patient Waiting Time," *Leadership in Health Services* 31, no. 3 (2018): 343-351, https://doi.org/10.1108/LHS-03-2018-0016.
539 George et al., *Lean Six Sigma Pocket Toolbook*.
540 Podsakoff et al., "Transformational Leader Behaviors and Follower Trust."
541 Ibid.
542 Kitchen and Daly, "Internal Communication during Change Management."
543 Trabucchi et al., "Sharing Economy: Seeing through the Fog."

of any pre-leadership or pre-accountability orientation or development:[544] Technical performance versus leadership has been the historical criterion for the jump from follower to leader status. This lack of skills development in seeing typically follows the leader through time unless a specific effort to orient the leader or the leadership team is undertaken.[545] The sections that follow are intended to be the dirty hands busted knuckle practical exposure to overcoming this skills deficit with the understanding both self-development and mentoring are required to fully develop understanding of the techniques.[546] The author's caveat is included before reading further – once you learn to see in this manner you will never be able to un-see again: Visits to McDonalds and other places of process chaos will both frustrate and enthrall you while driving through a Chick-Fil-A will make you smile.

Conflict Cloud

The Theory of Constraints uses the Conflict Cloud to depict the inherent tension between two opposing issues that cannot exist at the same time,[547] e.g., the desire for process standardization and process flexibility within the same entity. This type tension always underlies the core problem facing the leader as invariably the tension generates undesirable effects across the system.[548] The

---

544 Caligiuri, *Cultural Agility*.
545 University of Tennessee, *AFSO21: Air Force Smart Ops for the 21st Century."*
546 Kilkelly, "Creating Leaders for Successful Change Management."
547 Anderson and Adams, *Mastering Leadership*.
548 From the author's notes taken during his certification in the Theory of Constraints Jonah program in 2010 at the AGI Goldratt Institute. Presenters were Mr. Gerry Kendall and Mr. Bob Jacob.

Conflict Cloud is generated as the leader works through this tension to distill the elemental conflict in the system and is used to generate discussion as to what the organization truly desires.[549] If successful, the leader can use the Conflict Cloud as the first step in gaining buy-in to develop a solution to the conflict.[550] The Conflict Cloud directly postures the leader to begin the questioning steps in TOC's Thinking Process, i.e., what to change, what to change to, and how to cause the change.[551] The tension depicted in the Conflict Cloud highlights the core issues facing the leader, e.g., per the above, standardization or flexibility.[552] The Conflict Cloud helps simplify complexity[553] as it allows the leader to better see the system dynamics in play.[554] Of note, the Conflict Cloud can be used at the micro or macro levels to simplify the leader's focus and understanding of undesirable effects within a system which, in the instant case, is focused on better seeing what is on-going within organizational processes.[555]

---

549 Author's notes.
550 Ibid.
551 Ibid.
552 Ibid.
553 Manson, "Simplifying Complexity."
554 Meadows, *Dancing with Systems*.
555 Author's notes.

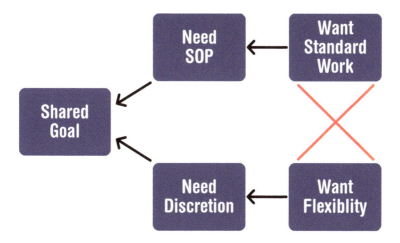

Figure 17: TOC Conflict Cloud

Value Stream Mapping (VSM)

The VSM technique is a deliberate effort to map the entire value stream of a process. As discussed above this would include the entire SIPOC (supplier, input, process, output, and customer) interface.[556] Subsequent to mapping the SIPOC interface the leader should work through the process from the customer end to the supplier end to check process logic then reverse course to recheck from supplier to customer.[557] Invariably, this dual end-to-end logic review approach will highlight value stream issues and concerns that can be targeted if changes add value to the customer.[558] Very specifically, the VSM identifies material and information flow through the value stream.[559]

---

556 George et al., *Lean Six Sigma Pocket Toolbook*.
557 Hershman, "Harnessing the Power of Process."
558 David Spear and D. Daly, "Lean Leader," *Simpler*, (2010). Note: This was part of the author's journey to expand beyond Lean Green Belt and was linked to the above Process Master effort. David Spear was the author's sensei during this period of professional development.
559 George et al., *Lean Six Sigma Pocket Toolbook*.

The leader gains critical knowledge from this exercise as visualization provides deeper awareness of issues and insights that should lead to a future state effort to improve.[560]

When the initial VSM is completed and the process logic has been reviewed the leader should conduct two subsequent steps. First, the VSM process logic likely has highlighted the need for buffers to control the work inputs into various process steps.[561] This is the application of the drum, buffer, rope aspects of TOC as the process flow and throughput rhythm is understood.[562] This focuses the leader on customer requirements and cash flow via revenue generation which is of paramount concern.[563] Second, the leader can focus on Lean Six Sigma concerns, i.e., the identification of non-value-added work, typically the various wastes discussed earlier, and process variation.[564] A key take-away is the VSM event is typically not a one-time effort. The author has supported one client who went through more than 50 VSMs on the same value stream as continuous improvement was the goal. This client linked the VSM events to an S-Curve[565] calendar which will be overviewed in a different section below.

---

560 Spear and Daly, "Lean Leader."
561 Eby, "Theory of Constraints."
562 Chakravorty and Atwater, "How Theory of Constraints can be used."
563 Kettering Global, "Theory of Constraints."
564 Eby, "Lean Six Sigma."
565 Ghorbani, "The Philosophy behind S-Curves."

Gemba Walk

A simple yet powerful leader tool is the Gemba walk. The Gemba walk can be formal or informal; however, the key is the leader literally goes to the place where the work is done to observe and interact with those doing the work in a respectful manner.[566] The leader's focus is on the process itself as the work is performed. The intent is for the leader to observe very carefully to see how work enters the process, how the process design performs, query the members on various aspects of the process, and as necessary to implement change.[567] Gemba means the 'real place' so it truly provides the leader a real-time opportunity to see the reality of the work underway.[568]

Figure 18: The Gemba Walk

---

566 Kanbanize, "Gemba Walk: Where the Real Work Happens," Kanban Software for Agile Project Management, (n.d.), https://kanbanize.com/lean-management/improvement/gemba-walk.

567 Shore, *Launching and Leading Change Initiatives in Health Care Organizations*.

568 Ibid.

Gemba walks are not designed to be cursory visits. This is a leader event that, even if informal, is intended to give the leader time to watch work being performed real-time.[569] This observation, this seeing, helps the leader see constraints, bottlenecks, and waste in the workflow and provides valuable insight into problem solving.

This seeing provides insight that can literally set the stage for subsequent moonshot type innovation and change which is the intent. Regardless of planned or unplanned, scripts exist to help the leader conduct effective Gemba walks. A key take-away is Gemba walks can prevent the inevitable efforts to filter information that reaches the leader as personal observation is undertaken. The live Gemba walk also provides the leader personal awareness how work is actually performed as opposed to how it should be done per a desk reference guide, a standard operating procedure, or some other type operating instruction.[570] This direct observation provides the leader insight into how incremental change may have crept into a process[571] as well as serving as the launch pad into a bold future state initiative.[572] The Gemba walk serves to bolster the leader's deeper understanding and knowledge of the work underway.[573]

Visual Management

This technique is the ultimate approach in rapidly assessing a process' performance in that key elements are

---

569 Kanbanize, "Gemba Walk: Where the Real Work Happens."
570 Sarantopoulos et al., "Using Lean Tools to Reduce Patient Waiting Time."
571 Anderson, *Organizational Development*.
572 Diamandis and Kotler, *Bold: How to Go Big*.
573 Kanbanize, "Gemba Walk: Where the Real Work Happens."

literally tracked visually and tell the process' story immediately assuming performance data are current.[574] Simple production control boards, or variations thereof, are maintained and used to calibrate process performance by the process members.[575] The SPC chart discussed earlier is the critical visual management tool for an immediate snapshot perspective.[576] Every Lean Six Sigma consultant will stress the need for Visual Management[577] yet many in leadership are unaware of this approach and many who use it do not maintain data currency so the technique quickly loses its power.

A secondary use for Visual Management is to simplify complexity.[578] The author has used Visual Management in this manner to support various clients with great success. In one example the client's work team had a text-based standard operating procedure (SOP) that was hundreds of pages long. Customer Service Representatives (CSR) were bogged down with ever present non-socialized changes in the SOP. The author, working with the CSR, implemented a 12-page visual management approach that could be rapidly updated and that increased speed of support while increasing accuracy. Leaders should become adept at Visual Management techniques given the typical requirements to leverage information.[579]

---

574 George et al., *Lean Six Sigma Pocket Toolbook*.
575 Ibid.
576 Hills, "Statistical Process Control Basic Control Charts."
577 George et al., *Lean Six Sigma Pocket Toolbook*.
578 Manson, "Simplifying Complexity."
579 Meadows, Leverage Points.

Metrics: The Critical Few

Big Data has overwhelmed many with the proliferation of analytics[580] and supporting tools such as Tableau and Smartsheet. Each has its place, but overload is common as leaders have access to every conceivable aspect of their operation at hand even as they are paralyzed by how to proceed.[581] This aspect of Big Data is commonly referred to as paralysis by analysis. In the Army and Marine Corps decision making systems commanders have what is known as the Commander's Critical Information Requirements (CCIR) to negate this phenomenon. These are the key data that, when triggered, are so important that the commander is immediately notified given the CCIR are invariably linked to a pre-planned decision point. Those who support the commander manage the multitude of Information Requirements specific to their portfolio but if a CCIR manifests the commander is immediately engaged.

The adoption of CCIR equivalents would benefit many in the non-military environment. As an example these could be renamed CEO Critical Information Requirements to ensure all supporting functions understood their importance. This would be a mental paradigm shift for many. From the author's perspective three key metrics attach to the CCIR metaphor. As always many will disagree;

---

580 Richard Vidgen, Sarah Shaw, and David B. Grant, "Management Challenges in Creating Value from Business Analytics" *European Journal of Operational Research* 261, no. 2 (2017): 626–39, https://doi.org/10.1016/j.ejor.2017.02.023.

581 Randy Bartlett, *A Practitioner's Guide to Business Analytics: Using Data Analysis Tools to Improve Your Organization's Decision Making and Strategy* (New York: Mcgraw-Hill, 2013).

however, disagreement at least means one has begun thinking through how to use this approach.

Inventory Turn. Inventory Turn is normally associated with retail or other organizations that hold inventory and speaks to the ratio of cost of goods sold to inventory.[582] If the reader recalls, inventory is part of the Theory of Constraints approach to global accounting and is considered a cost driver.[583] As such, the goal is to reduce inventory quickly via the velocity-based approach to throughput.[584] Inventory Turn is a down and dirty metric that immediately addresses profitability or effectiveness of the process in play.[585]

In administrative and transactional organizations the leader can adapt Inventory Turn to whatever the work is, e.g., in the HR office area processing actions can be tracked via this metric with great success. The key is to educate the members on the concept,[586] e.g., first defining what the metric is[587] and then using a metaphor or analogy to help the members understand.[588] The author has used Amazon selling shoes as an example given most everyone knows how quickly Amazon delivers. The concept resonates with most as they can mentally visualize the action to be worked as a box of shoes that must be moved rapidly else the inventory cost eats into any

---

582 Francesca Nicasio, "Inventory Turnover 101: What It Is and How to Get It Right," Vend Retail Blog, May 11, 2021, https://www.vendhq.com/blog/inventory-turnover/.
583 Kettering Global, "Theory of Constraints."
584 Jacob et al., *Velocity*.
585 Nicasio, "Inventory Turnover 101."
586 Will and Pies, "Sensemaking and Sensegiving."
587 Nicasio, "Inventory Turnover 101."
588 Morgan, *Images of Organizations*.

profit. Once this is accomplished the organization is one step closer to the desired velocity-based approach to throughput[589] which, again, is universal in its approach.

First Pass Yield. This metric, First Pass Yield (FPY),[590] is both a quality-oriented metric and a financial metric as it very directly addresses whether work went through the process with no errors or required rework. The FPY metric is binary as each item going through the process passes or fails per the process performance criteria. This metric has multiple nuances but for purposes of this section it is offered as means to identify what, to many, is an unrecognized cost, i.e., the cost of rework due to errors in processing. From the author's experience many in leadership and in followership roles dislike the application of this metric due to its binary nature and to the fact that it not only is a cost indicator but can be used to evaluate leader, member, and process performance simultaneously. As such, many fear it once it is implemented.

The FPY metric is applicable to all processes. For those in a profit-oriented organization this can be used to identify process issues that eat into margin and for service-oriented organizations it can be an opportunity to improve before the customer seeks another source. In all instances it can also be a measure of technical competence. The FPY metric is powerful; however, like the Inventory Turn metric, must be socialized before

---

589 Jacob et al., *Velocity*.
590 Matthew L. Littlefield, "Manufacturing Metrics: First Pass Yield Benchmark Data," January 24, 2013, Manufacturing Metrics: First Pass Yield Benchmark Data (lnsresearch.com). Note: The author has used First Pass Yield in numerous instances but desired a citation to verify the approach.

implementation to ensure member awareness of its intended uses. It can be punitive in nature which is not the author's intent.

Pareto Analysis. The Pareto Analysis is integral to the Total Quality Management approach[591] and is also used in Lean Six Sigma as it highlights performance drivers, errors, or variability depending upon intent and usage.[592] The Pareto Analysis allows the leader to immediately focus on the top drivers to gain maximum value or leverage.[593] The Pareto Analysis is also known as the 80-20 rule which speaks to how the leader spends time and resources for the most benefit.[594] The Pareto Analysis, if used routinely, will provide the leader a real-time window into the performance drivers as well as the impediments to performance depending upon how set up. The key is to understand the power of the 80-20 rule and to use your energy and resources to leverage[595] throughput to maximize revenue generation or service provision.[596]

The Pareto Analysis not only helps target process performance for improvement.[597] It also serves as a means to influence organizational member performance as most members pay attention to what the leader is monitoring.[598] The leader can allow this to be subtle or much more direct depending upon numerous variables,

---

591 Motzko, "Deming's 14 Points for Management."
592 Ted Hessing, "Pareto Analysis," 6σstudyguide.com, (n.d.), Pareto Analysis | Six Sigma Study Guide.
593 Meadows, *Leverage Points*.
594 Motzko, "Deming's 14 Points for Management."
595 Meadows, *Leverage Points*.
596 Kettering Global, "Theory of Constraints."
597 Sobek and Smalley, *Understanding A3 thinking*.
598 Ibid.

e.g., member skill and competency levels, stakeholder input, time constraints, etc. The Pareto Analysis can be the genesis for continued improvement and innovation as the performance drivers are understood.[599]

Data Management and Dashboards

The Visual Management and Metric discussion above segue into the leader's need for a visual dashboard with drill down capability in the event the leader needs to parse the underlying data; however, if designed correctly the critical information will already be displayed.[600] The dashboard should be as simple as possible to preclude the inclusion of non-critical inputs. Support staff need to be trained, coached, and mentored on why the critical few metrics are deemed critical and to alert the leader if changes occur that could trigger opportunities or that serve as warning of pending problems. The leader dashboard needs to be monitored at least daily to ensure real-time awareness.

A second caveat on data management is to track work that leaves the leader's control but that is important to work completion, e.g., in some transactional processes the organization is dependent upon input from people outside the organization to complete forms or provide other information required for the process to continue.[601] When this information leaves the organization the workflow progress is now out of the leader's control as a dependency arises. This is a parking lot that must be

---

599 Ibid.
600 Stephanie Evergreen, "Presenting Data Effectively," Archived Webinar, 2017, SAGE Publishing.
601 George et al., *Lean Six Sigma Pocket Toolbook*.

managed for situational awareness during the dependency period. If the outside agent returns the required information it should be re-entered into a control buffer and released per the next process step's capacity to produce the work.[602] The author typically recommends this type of buffer be used to control the release into the next process step via a First In-First Out technique to enhance process velocity.[603] If not managed this type work invariably generates discord and confusion as well as backlog which are avoidable undesirable effects.[604]

THE S-CURVE IMPROVEMENT APPROACH

The S-Curve improvement technique is wedded to the Statistical Process Control (SPC) chart described earlier.[605] The S-Curve approach is a means for pre-planned changes for the organization that desires stability yet understands improvements must be made to the wash, rinse, repeat mantra to remain competitive.[606] The S-Curve is linked to the SPC chart via the use of the upper and lower control lines, i.e., as the pre-planned change occurs the current upper control limit becomes the lower control limit in the future state, or, the S-Curve is linked to a pre-planned decision to reduce variability by reducing the control limits to tighten performance expectations.[607] Either approach sets the expectation

---

602 Eby, "Theory of Constraints."
603 Jacob et al., *Velocity*.
604 Eby, "Theory of Constraints."
605 Ghorbani, "The Philosophy Behind S-Curves."
606 Hammel, *Leading the Revolution*.
607 Motzko, "Deming's 14 Points for Management."

that performance is intended to become more efficient. This approach is only applicable as the organization's processes reach the center and right of the Squiggly Line and the focus on efficiency makes sense/cents.[608]

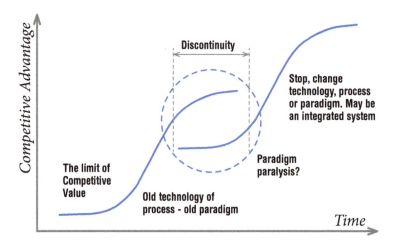

Figure 19: The S-Curve

There is both art and science involved with the S-Curve technique that is well worth the time learning given it may be used with every organizational process to ensure continual improvement occurs in every area.[609] The schedule approach embeds a battle rhythm or cadence within the organization that sets the pace of controlled incremental changes designed to improve macro performance pending any radical innovative effort.[610] This approach

---

608 Jacob et al., *Velocity*.

609 Marcelo Bronzo, Paulo Tarso Vilela de Resende, Marcos Paulo Valadares de Oliveira, Kevin P. McCormack, Paulo Renato de Sousa, and Reinaldo Lopes Ferreira, "Improving Performance Aligning Business Analytics with Process Orientation," *International Journal of Information Management* 33, no. 2 (2013): 300–307, https://doi.org/10.1016/j.ijinfomgt.2012.11.011.

610 Hammel, *Leading the Revolution*.

precludes the tendency to suboptimize performance. The key is to ensure the organizational members working the process are aware of the S-Curve schedule, e.g., changes to occur every 90 days, to ensure time for input, new resources, retraining, BMCing, etc., that must be addressed. Note this is directly related to the C+7™ change management approach also discussed earlier as well as to the caveat about the point of diminishing return...art and science are in play as the leader balances the pressures of effectiveness versus efficiency against successful change.[611]

EXECUTION TOOL: THE A3

There are numerous execution tools available to leaders, e.g., the military has used decision support matrices for years; however, the best tool to help simplify change management complexity the author has encountered is the A3.[612] This tool originated with Toyota and contains a true executive summary of most any plan in that the user must reduce the plan to fit onto one page, the A3. The contents include a description of the issue, the current state, the desired future state, a gap analysis between the two, and steps to make the transition.[613]

Note the schematic or picture is the superficial aspect of the A3; the thinking behind it is its real value as the leader must deeply think through the issue in order to reduce concepts and concerns to one page.[614] As an

---

[611] Alan H. Church, "The Art and Science of Evaluating Organization Development Interventions," *OD Practitioner* 49, no. 2 (2017): 26-35.
[612] Sobek and Smalley, *Understanding A3 Thinking*.
[613] Ibid.
[614] Ibid.

example, the S-Curve reflects the *what to* be changed whereas the A3 can be configured as the *how to cause* the changes. The A3 can be strategic for an organization's ten-year plan or it can be tailored as an individual's personal development plan. It is as versatile as it is powerful. Figure 20 reflects the author's second-generation farm A3. He is reflecting upon the fourth generation.

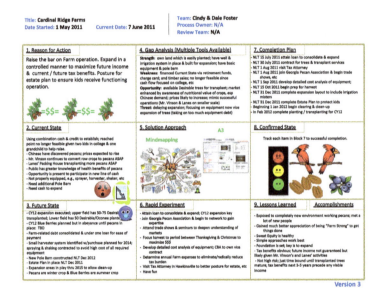

Figure 20: The Author's Farm A3

AUTOPSY FAILURES

Elon Musk epitomizes learning from failure. As the author is drafting this section Mr. Musk has just provided the public insight into why Starship SN11 crashed its planned landing. This is a recurring event with Mr. Musk as he is pushing the envelope on rocketry innovation, i.e., he is using rapid inventory turns to prototype his Starship effort and is conducting rapid analysis of his failures as he prepares his next effort.[615] He is failing fast as he literally is attempting a Mars shot instead of a bold moonshot.[616] There are leadership lessons embedded in his often-humorous Twitter replies to questions, e.g., he is transparent both in his failures and in his rapid analysis as to why. In many cases transparency may not be the best approach given the need to protect proprietary information for competitive advantage yet the autopsy approach is readily importable to any organization. As in the more common understanding of autopsy failure forensics can provide the leader valuable insights that can be applied to the next effort. This is a rich source for not only improvement but for next level innovation.[617]

SUMMARY

- Learning to see differently is a critical leader requirement if effectiveness if the goal.
- Multiple tools exist to help the leader see. Those depicted have universal applicability.
- Big Data can be and often is overwhelming. The leader should focus on the critical few metrics that drive decisions. Support staff should be responsible for all others.
- The leader imperative accepts that change is inevitable. Planning for change via the S-Curve, at a minimum, postures the leader to stay ahead of the curve.

---

615 Yanqing Duan, Guangming Cao, and John S. Edwards, "Understanding the Impact of Business Analytics on Innovation," *European Journal of Operational Research*, (June 2018), https://doi.org/10.1016/ejor.2018.06.021.

616 Diamandis and Kotler, *Bold: How to Go Big*.

617 Ibid.

- Executing change is often problematic. The distilled A3, built after deep thought and analysis, simplifies the complexity of managing change.
- Failure will happen. Learn from it. Exploit it. Do not focus on it except as a learning vehicle.

Section IV: Integration

Ultimately, leaders are choreographers of people and processes regardless of the organization's mission or purpose. If either is missing or mistimed for whatever reason the organization's effectiveness is impacted as the organization is a system instead of autonomous siloed components.[618] Concurrent with the choreographical issues leaders are influencers who directly or indirectly affect organizational performance via their holistic or 360 degree interactions with stakeholders, suppliers, superiors, peers, and subordinates.[619] This duality, i.e., choreography and influence, is critical at any given time but is vital whenever organizations seek planned changes and/or innovation.[620] Such simply will not happen successfully without direct leader engagement and without leader understanding of the dynamics in play.[621]

The final chapters of *Dirty Hands Busted Knuckles* attempt to integrate the earlier chapters into a holistic perspective. As always, many will find weaknesses or flaws to the author's approach but again this difference in perspective simply means the reader is thinking through

---

[618] George et al., *Lean Six Sigma Pocket Toolbook*.
[619] Cialdini, *Influence*.
[620] Hammel, *Leading the Revolution*.
[621] Ho Wook Shin, Joseph C. Picken, and Gregory G. Dess, "Revisiting the Learning Organization: How to Create It," *Organizational Dynamics* 46 (2017): 46-56.

the implications.[622] Goodness is occurring which is the author's intent.

---

[622] CDC, "The Value of Systems Thinking, YouTube, 2017, https://www.youtube.com/watch?v=Fo3ndxVOZEo&feature=youtu.be.

Chapter 9. Braiding the Rope

"Leadership is unlocking people's potential to become better".[623]

The author has encountered numerous people in leadership positions who likely should not have been or who should have been culled early because of the harm done. In many cases this was because the person was not adept or skilled in handling people, e.g., they did not have the know-how to deal with conflict, or because they solely focused on the technical components of the organization leaving the organizational members in a state of inattention. In any of these situations the organization suffers as do the organizational members who typically are aware of the lack of integration of people and processes.[624] Leadership is choreography but more importantly it is the integration of people and processes into a system oriented to the organization's purpose that matters.[625] And, as importantly, the leader's understanding of how that

---

[623] Kevin Kruse, "100 Best Quotes on Leadership," Forbes, Accessed June 21, 2021, https://www.forbes.com/sites/kevinkruse/2012/10/16/quotes-on-leadership/?sh=38a9f3102feb.

[624] Paul Nelissen and Martine van Selm, "Surviving Organizational Change: How Management Communication Helps Balance Mixed Feelings," *Corporate Communications: An International Journal* 13, no. 3 (2008): 306-318, https://doi.org/10/1108/13563280810893670.

[625] Jamie Vernon, "Understanding the Butterfly Effect," *American Scientist* 105, no. 3 (2107):130, https://doi.org/10.1511/2017.105.3.130.

system works at the macro level is vital.[626] The following sections highlight these organizational dynamics that many in leadership seemingly miss.

CONFLUENCE

The author is intentionally using two metaphors in this chapter, i.e., braiding the rope and confluence.[627] The individual strands of people and process are virtually worthless due to the interdependencies required for performance hence the need to braid them into a strong rope to gain the synergy of integration; however, like two rivers joining the leader can expect turbulence as the braiding occurs given the need to also integrate the two into a seamless effort.[628] The confluence of people and process is often very turbulent as people naturally resist change[629] and yet, to sustain competitive advantage, both people and processes invariably must be improved to maintain, much less gain, new workload. Figure 21 depicts this confluence of people and process.

---

626 Hammel, *Leading the Revolution*.
627 Morgan, *Images of Organizations*.
628 Brubaker et al., "Conflict Resolution."
629 Oster, "Listening to Luddites."

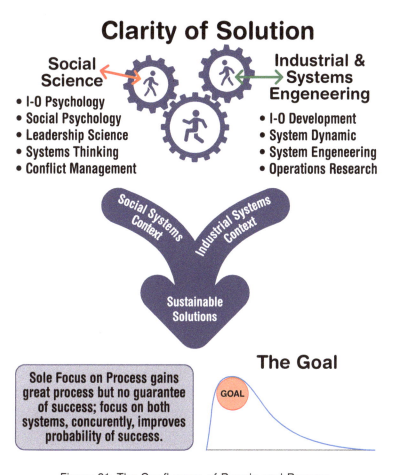

Figure 21: The Confluence of People and Process

The leader's presence is vital to overcoming this turbulence hence the need for the leader to be well versed in vision casting, communicating, and resolving all manner of conflict that will be present.[630] At a more fundamental level the leader must be able to anticipate both people and process issues to ensure individual personal issues are resolved concurrent with resolving process flow issues. The leader must be adroit and adept in the

---
630 Sosik and Jung, *Full Range Leadership Development*.

fundamentals of human behavior and organizational behavior as well as process management regardless of the nature of the organization.[631] In effect, these leader skills are required in, and exportable to, any organization.

RIPPLES

The astute leader will be attuned to not only the above concerns but also to how even the most minute change in an organization can have large impact.[632] Many in leadership, especially at the lower to middle levels and in the staff functions, often do not understand the organization as a whole and are blind to how a seemingly simple policy change can generate unanticipated negativity.[633] Figure 22 depicts what is commonly known as the McKinsey 7-S Framework.[634] This model depicts the high-level interrelationships between and among the most common organizational characteristics. All leaders would do well to understand this phenomenon and to factor it into their decision making, sense-giving, and change management processes.[635] Failure to do so will generate undesirable effects that could have been avoided.[636] Note this is inextricably linked to both planned and unplanned changes

---

631 Jie Wang, Grand H. L. Cheng, Tingting Chen, and Kwok Leung, "Team Creativity/Innovation in Culturally Diverse Teams: A Meta-Analysis," *Journal of Organizational Behavior* 40, no. 6 (2019): 693–708, https://doi.org/10.1002/job.2362.

632 Vernon, "Understanding the Butterfly Effect."

633 M. Levin, "The Top 10 Leadership Blind Spots, and 5 Ways to Turn Them into Strengths," Inc.com, July 13, 2017, The Top 10 Leadership Blind Spots, and 5 Ways to Turn Them Into Strengths | Inc.com.

634 McKinsey and Company, "Enduring Ideas: The 7-S Framework," McKinsey Quarterly, March 1, 2008, Enduring Ideas: The 7-S Framework | McKinsey.

635 Will and Pies, "Sensemaking and Sensegiving."

636 Kettering Global, "Theory of Constraints."

as well as for all innovation efforts and speaks directly to the organization being deemed ready for change.[637]

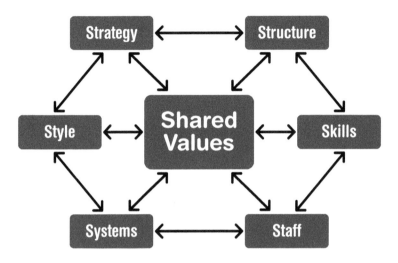

Figure 22: McKinsey 7-S Framework

A second area that will cause unexpected ripples relates to the interdependence of process and people.[638] The leader must be aware that most process practitioners and staff entities do not recognize the engagement levels of the employees who actually do the work when helping the organization determine how the processes should be staffed, i.e., in determining the number of Full Time Equivalents required to execute the work.[639] As such, the computations used to determine manning requirements are invariably wrong due to the implicit assumption employee engagement is 100 percent, e.g., if the process math indicates three people are required in a subtask but

---

637 Hammel, Leading the Revolution.
638 Anderson and Adams, *Mastering Leadership*.
639 George et al. *Lean Six Sigma Pocket Toolbook*.

each is only 40 percent engaged the work will not be accomplished per pre-planned budget and schedule. This is an inherit weakness in most modeling approaches as modeling is a hard skill typically administered by technical personnel not usually versed in or oriented to the human element. This is an inherent but unrecognized part of the daily math requirement discussed earlier; ensure you are using a complete formula.[640] It is here that leadership encounters the aforementioned turbulence as the difference in performance levels must be addressed somehow. And it is here that the leader's conflict management skills rise to the surface, or not, as employees will be expected to overcome the lack of production by their unengaged or actively disengaged peers.

As a leader, one must always integrate people into the process and part of that integration is knowing this data point.[641] The key take-away is knowing engagement levels is of no value if this knowledge is not integrated into the macro system ergo the value of understanding Figure 18, the McKinsey 7-S Framework.[642] Overcoming this likely oversight is a different matter, a political matter in most cases.[643]

---

640 Ibid.
641 Sosik and Jung, *Full Range Leadership Development*.
642 Anderson and Adams, *Mastering Leadership*.
643 Kelsey Dappa, Feyza Bhatti, and Ahmad Aljarah, "A Study on the Effect of Transformational Leadership on Job Satisfaction: The Role of Gender, Perceived Organizational Politics and Perceived Organizational Commitment," *Management Science Letters*, (2019): 823-834, https://doi.org/10.5267/j.msl.2019.3.006.

POLITICS: THE ANTITHESIS OF COMMITMENT

The discussion above is one aspect of organizational politics in that, within the leadership team, it is common for leaders to jockey for position via the budget and other management control systems.[644] Relative to the above the leader with this conundrum must exert direct and indirect influence[645] and negotiate to overcome the impact.[646] Good luck.

In the interim just clearly understand that a secondary aspect of organizational politics concerns its impact on overall performance.[647] The perception of politics, i.e., the perception that the leader plays favorites, generates hostility and what in academic terms is known as counterproductive workplace behaviors.[648] For the highly engaged, highly committed employees politics is a cancer that destroys what the organization supposedly wants – loyal, committed, highly productive employees who are intrinsically motivated.[649]

In the People section above much space was given to the consideration of developing positive relationships with all organizational members.[650] That admonition is thematic within this book even though in most organizations there are readily visible in- and out-groups.[651]

---

644 Sosik and Jung, *Full Range Leadership Development*.
645 United States, *Army leadership: Competent, Confident, and Agile*.
646 Roger Fisher, William Ury, and Bruce Patton, *Getting to Yes: Negotiating Agreement Without Giving In* (New York, NY: Houghton Mifflin, 1991).
647 Meisler et al., "Perceived Organizational Politics."
648 Meisler et al., "Perceived Organizational Politics."
649 Pickford and Joy, "Organizational Citizenship Behaviours."
650 Sosik and Jung, *Full Range Leadership Development*.
651 Northouse, *Leadership*.

When coupled with the mere perception of politics the leader faces a maelstrom of potential destructive behaviors that result from the overt hostility generated.[652] The link between hostility and destructive behaviors to the perception of politics is well researched.[653] The leader must decide which is more valuable, i.e., politics or the benefits that result from the positivity of high-quality relationships.[654] There is a natural tension or polarity between the two that cannot be resolved and that directly affects organizational alignment.[655]

Figure 23 depicts the work environment and the intersection of negative and positive organizational citizenship behaviors.[656] Many to the left of the mean, the unengaged and the actively disengaged, can be rehabilitated and converted to productive organizational members. The leader simply must know the environment and understand what prompted these two groups to locate where they are. Perception matters, and if in the out-group, favoritism and politics are common themes of discontent.[657]

---

[652] Meisler et al., "Perceived Organizational Politics."

[653] Ibid.

[654] Rokeach, *The Nature of Human Values*, (New York: NY, Free Press, 1973).

[655] Anderson and Adams, *Mastering Leadership*.

[656] Yongxing Guo, Haiyang Kang, Bo Shao, and Beni Halvorsen, "Organizational Politics as a Blindfold," *Personnel Review* 48, no. 3 (2019): 784-798, https://doi.org/10.1108/pr-07-2017-0205.

[657] Guo et al., "Organizational Politics as a Blindfold."

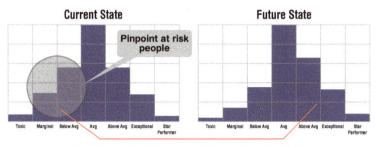

Figure 23: Recovering the Disengaged Employees

ALIGNMENT

The leader's choreography and influence should be oriented to alignment of all efforts to the organization's vision and goals.[658] Efforts not aligned cost the organization effectiveness and margin.[659] It is as simple as that. The leader who does not give due diligence to all aspects of the organization contributes to alignment issues.[660] It is therefore an imperative that the leader master the skills for both people and process to ensure effectiveness: Leaders simply do not have the latitude to focus singularly on people or on process as both are required for success.[661] Nor can the leader allow silos to exist as they invariably allow for optimizing silo performance at the expense of organizational performance.[662] See Figure 24. These are the components of organizational behavior

---

658 Kouzes and Posner, *The Leadership Challenge*.
659 Kettering Global, "Theory of Constraints."
660 United States, *Army leadership: Competent, Confident, and Agile*.
661 Anderson and Adams, *Mastering Leadership*.
662 George et al., *Lean Six Sigma Pocket Toolbook*.

that leaders must not only understand but master as nuances matter.[663]

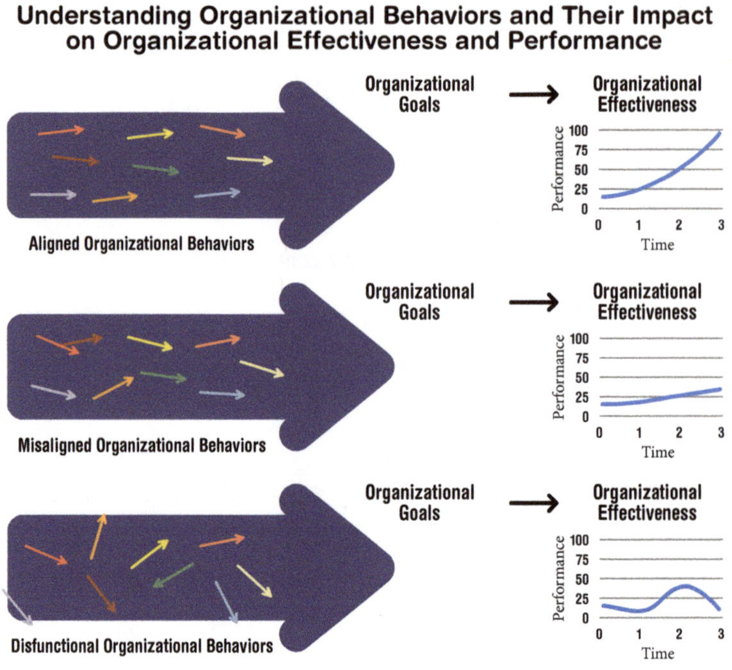

Understanding Organizational Behaviors and Their Impact on Organizational Effectiveness and Performance

Aligned Organizational Behaviors → Organizational Goals → Organizational Effectiveness

Misaligned Organizational Behaviors → Organizational Goals → Organizational Effectiveness

Disfunctional Organizational Behaviors → Organizational Goals → Organizational Effectiveness

Figure 24: The Stages of Organizational Behavior

SYSTEMS DYNAMICS

If one integrates people and process per the above, and if one considers Figure 25, the McKinsey 7-S Framework, one should begin to see the organization as an organized system instead of a set of discrete business units or workstreams.[664] The McKinsey 7-S Framework depicts this systemic perspective and allows the leader to better

---

663 Daniels, *Performance Management*.
664 Draper L. Kauffman, *Systems One: An Introduction to Systems Thinking* (The Future Systems Series, 1980).

understand the interactive nature of systems and how the interactive components provide feedback if one is paying attention.[665] It is this systems perspective that provides the leader the ability to better understand how resistance occurs as individual members and groups attempt to maintain continuity and stability versus necessarily or readily accepting change or innovation.[666]

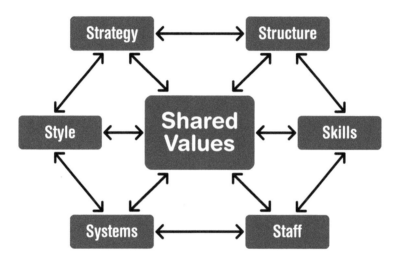

Figure 25: The McKinsey 7-2 Framework

It is this point that many in leadership fail to understand when attempting change or innovation, i.e., that the system seeks stability first and foremost and that to effect a change the members within the system must be addressed instead of simply attempting the change via brute force; typically an indirect approach to change is best and that only after careful consideration of the

---

665 Draper, *Systems One: An Introduction to Systems Thinking*.
666 Ibid.

system.[667] Arguably, in the case of organizations, the system and the culture minimally overlap and may actually be the same but that is the topic for a different book.[668]

Leaders seeking breakthrough performance via innovation[669] must understand how to negate the system preference for stability in order to amplify the benefits of affective commitment and organizational citizenship behaviors that result therefrom.[670] In order to amplify this goodness the leader must focus on, and leverage,[671] the power of high-quality relationships within an organization as free from the perception of politics as possible.[672] Conversely, if the leader sees an organization undergoing the wreckage of counterproductive workplace behaviors the leader must undertake a systems approach to break that cycle also.[673] Again, the most obvious, the most direct approach may generate a worsened environment.[674] Think systems and leverage when you reflect, ponder, and plan your way ahead.[675]

SUMMARY

- Leadership requires the full integration of people and process. This integration invariably generates friction and conflict.

---

667 Ibid.
668 Morgan, *Images of Organizations*.
669 Anderson and Adams, *Mastering Leadership*.
670 Kauffman, *Systems One: An Introduction to Systems Thinking*.
671 Meadows, *Dancing with Systems*.
672 Meisler et al., "Perceived Organizational Politics."
673 Kauffman, *Systems One: An Introduction to Systems Thinking*.
674 Ibid.
675 Wang et al., "The Effects of Self-Reflection."

- A systems approach provides the leader the optimum perspective to factor in engagement, alignment, politics, and all the other variables that impact the organization.
- Look for leverage points to effect lasting change.
- Politics are the antithesis of affective commitment. Beware.

Chapter 10. Becoming: Things to Ponder

"Every act of creation is first of all an act of destruction".[676]

Volatility. Uncertainty. Complexity. Ambiguity. VUCA. These words and this acronym aptly describe the ever-more complex operating environment in which leaders must navigate.[677] The status quo may be desirable, even comfortable, but such an approach likely will not suffice very long before change must occur.[678] Many styles of leadership would not foresee this, or if forecasted, plan for it given the tendency for laissez-fair or management-by-exception leadership styles.[679] The transformational leader, however, operates differently. He or she understands the requirement for recurring adaptive behavior to not only anticipate change but to relish the opportunity to pull change forward to leverage it as a competitive advantage.[680] The transformational leader understands this VUCA environment requires constancy

---

[676] Anderson and Adams, *Mastering Leadership*.
[677] Bob, Johansen, *The New Leadership Literacies: Thriving in a Future of Extreme Disruption and Distributed Everything* (Berrett-Koehler Publishers, Inc, 2017).
[678] Hammel, *Leading the Revolution*.
[679] Sosik and Jung, *Full Range Leadership Development*.
[680] Anderson and Adams, *Mastering Leadership*.

of change simply to keep up: The transformational leader understands this simple but critical leadership imperative that enhances leadership effectiveness.[681]

LEADERSHIP ENGAGEMENT: KEY TO LEADERSHIP EFFECTIVENESS

Organizations that focus on an employee engagement metric are reacting to a symptom. Their illness is poor leader engagement. As a result, for decades, businesses and organizations have often languished as the employee engagement ratings hover at 70 percent unengaged or disengaged and cash has flowed to global consulting firms for help in remediating the symptom. The author has lived this as the project champion for implementing the world-renowned employee engagement survey for a large military industrial complex coupled with the complementary approach to strengths management. The author was rebuffed by senior and executive leadership that they were targeting the wrong audience even as the senior leadership team were very well versed and experienced in conducting root cause analysis for industrial operations. They failed to use the applicable tool as many were enamored with the consulting firm's reputation and prestige.

The strengths effort failed even though they had very good data and analysis for the root cause application. Consider that a 70 percent unengaged or disengaged workforce actually means only 30 percent of leadership is engaged and effective. Again, the basic classes in school for solving for 'x' are applicable; it becomes an

---
[681] Ibid.

issue of variable recognition and understanding how to leverage critical points for success.[682] For leadership effectiveness to increase leadership engagement must increase.[683] Leadership engagement means sleeves rolled up and hands-on efforts to align members to the organization's visions and goals.[684] The topics below address key aspects and techniques of leadership engagement that leaders should deliberately and affirmatively leverage at every opportunity; note each is an integral component of a leader engagement portfolio or system.[685]

VISION CASTING

From the process perspective identifying the desired future state is actually vision casting.[686] This is the crux of leadership effectiveness, i.e., setting the stage for all to see where you the leader intend to lead the organization.[687] Vision casting is elemental to leadership. The vision must be such that members know it is personal to the leader, i.e., the leader has skin in the game, and it must be audacious and lofty to the point members want to be party to its attainment[688] so do not hesitate to be bold to set the stage for breakthrough performance.[689] BHAG. Flying Pigs. Moonshots.

---

682 Meadows, *Leverage Points*.
683 Sosik and Jung, *Full Range Leadership Development*.
684 Kouzes and Posner, *The Leadership Challenge*.
685 Virginia Anderson and Lauren Johnson, *Systems Thinking Basics: From Concepts to Causal Loops* (Cambridge, MA: Pegasus Communications, 1997).
686 Podsakoff et al., "Transformational Leader Behaviors and Follower Trust."
687 Anderson and Adams, *Mastering Leadership*.
688 Ibid.
689 Diamandis and Kotler, *Bold: How to Go Big*.

A key consideration to remember is that your current organizational structure and internal systems are limiting factors.[690] As you set this moonshot vision in play, understand that you are setting the stage for everything to change. This is typically a key weakness in successful change simply because this is not a planning factor. Leaders seek transformation and breakthrough performance but forget the structural design and governance systems are set for status quo performance.[691]

A second elemental vision casting consideration is to understand that there are multiple futures possible.[692] As you set the moonshot vision, set in play multiple potential pathways to attain the vision.[693] In the military, commanders expect to see multiple courses of action (COA) designed to attain the objective. Within the COA that is selected as the way ahead planners have built in what are called branches and sequels that are based on pre-identified decision points. If the decision point analysis indicates facts and assumptions have changed, commanders may opt to execute a branch plan to leverage the new situation. Concurrently, when the objective is achieved the sequel planning provides a way ahead to the next objective. This approach anticipates multiple future scenarios. In fact, most military planning cells have a specific Future Planning team in play that is always looking well ahead of the current operation. You may not have the luxury of this type planning team; however,

---

690 Anderson and Adams, *Mastering Leadership*.
691 Ibid.
692 Chermack, *Scenario Planning*.
693 Ibid.

you should always be looking well ahead of today as you reflect upon the future. It may be disconcerting to those around you but thinking 6-12-18-36-60 months ahead should be your norm given the rapidity of change...the future is coming at you via a high rate of speed regardless of your readiness for it.[694] Leverage this simple fact. Build multiple possible futures into your vision casting using a long-term way over-the-horizon approach.[695] Concurrent with this approach, understand that the next elemental competency you need to leverage is communication.

COMMUNICATION

At the end of the day the leader's technical skills are important but likely are not vital to his or her success. Ultimately, the leader's success depends upon his or her competency in communicating with members.[696] Many fight this observation yet nothing gets done without communication in one of its various forms, e.g., face-to-face, emails, texts, phone calls, or written correspondence, and it is this communication expertise that distinguishes the effective leader as messaging occurs.[697] The effective communicator consciously or unconsciously understands the components of Emotional Intelligence, the power of storytelling, and knows that his or her communicative efforts enhance buy-in and alignment; it is within the communication domain that the skills and attributes of

---

[694] Diamandis and Kotler, *Bold: How to Go Big*.
[695] Chermack, *Scenario Planning*.
[696] Murrar and Brauer, "Overcoming Resistance to Change."
[697] Denning, *The Secret Language of Leadership*.

the effective leader coalesce into a jetstream of influence, persuasion, and trust-building.[698]

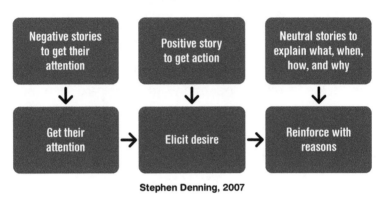

Figure 26: The Secret Language of Leadership

CULTURE TRUMPS STRATEGY

Read this subtitle over and over and over. Culture rules and its members will attempt to deflect, sabotage, and derail efforts to change the status quo if the culture is not oriented to change and innovation or if it has not been prepped for change.[699] Transformation is radical change ergo this admonition. The leader must understand the dynamics of culture[700] and its implications on all aspects of the organization.[701] This topic exceeds the parameters of this book; however, it should be a high interest item for every leader – knowing the current cultural type, the

---

698 Ibid.
699 Schneider, "Why Good Management Ideas Fail."
700 Hofstede et al., *Cultures and Organizations: Software of the Mind.*
701 Cameron and Quinn, *Diagnosing and Changing Organizational Culture.*

type's fit to the vision and goals, and how to implement cultural change are all critical factors in an environment that requires seemingly never-ending change.[702]

TRANSFORMATION

A quick Amazon search for transformational leadership books resulted in over 1,000 possibilities. Discussion of transformation is very popular yet in the author's experience such discussion is high-level and rhetorical with little practical value. You should read a lot of these books to broaden your knowledge; however, to make the shift from current state leadership style to that of the transformational leader you must combine learning with both intent and action to change.[703] This takes literal awareness of your current state hence the need for personal assessments and a concrete action plan. This is the power of the Personal Development A3, i.e., a simple but powerful awareness of your current state, a picture of the desired future state, acceptance of the gap, and very discrete but executable steps to migrate your style.[704]

Every day should include your personal action to affect the desired changes and an end-of-day reflection of your accomplishments.[705] Transformational change, even if personal, is a process and processes must be assessed and recalibrated as needed. The Personal Development A3 becomes your individualized Transformation Plan of Care as metamorphosis occurs by design.[706]

---

702 Ibid.
703 Scott Adams, "Goals vs. Systems," Scott Adams' Blog, 2013,
704 Sobek and Smalley, *Understanding A3 Thinking*.
705 Robertson, "The Stoicism of Benjamin Franklin."
706 Hershman, "Harnessing the Power of Process."

The Butterfly

There are numerous metaphors concerning change yet most people likely immediately recall their basic science classes where they learned how the lowly caterpillar encases itself in a cocoon, and while inside, basically dissolves with the resulting organic matter rearranging into the butterfly.[707] There is no going back and every observer is well aware that transformation has occurred. The prior form is left behind as the new form emerges. For the leader, this transformation occurs as the leader leaves earlier styles and attains the thinking and behaviors of the transformational leader.[708] Succinctly, this means the leader never again engages in avoidance of issues, and unless an almost life and death issue so requires, shows utter disdain for micromanagement.[709]

The Leader

As an undergraduate the author had the opportunity to live and study in Germany for three months to improve his German language skills. One of the most difficult requirements was to read and discuss Kafka's Metamorphosis completely auf Deutsch. A lot of time and effort was involved to get that passing grade. Concurrently, the author started dreaming in German. The author was far from native speaker competency but the click had occurred; nuances, idioms, and culture made better

---

707 Anderson and Adams, *Mastering Leadership*.
708 Sosik and Jung, *Full Range Leadership Development*.
709 Ibid.

sense. The author's mental model had begun to transform relative to language acquisition.[710]

To be a transformational leader you must undergo a similar shift in learning and thinking to truly leverage the power of leader engagement and leader effectiveness.[711] The section above, The Butterfly, is germane as you too must radically morph[712]... think religious conversion, a death and resurrection level event that you must undergo to reach the level where people see and experience you in an idealized manner, a level of leadership wherein you both inspire and motivate as your every interaction is personalized and influential.[713] Remember, as a leader every engagement, every conversation is both a negotiation and an opportunity to more deeply align individuals to the organization's vision.[714] Every engagement. Every conversation. Master communication competencies and understand how influence and persuasion work...there is a method to the madness that can be leveraged for goodness instead of manipulation.[715]

Butterflies may not be your thing but their elegance is a thing of beauty to behold as is their power to affect change.[716] Unless you as an individual leader morph the chances of any organizational transformation being successful are almost nil – remember, the research indicates

---

[710] Lawrence, "Leading Change."
[711] Gilbert, "The Psychology of Your Future Self."
[712] Goldstein, "The Battle between Your Present and Future Self."
[713] Sosik and Jung, *Full Range Leadership Development*.
[714] Senge, *The Fifth Discipline Fieldbook*.
[715] Cialdini, *Influence*.
[716] Vernon, "Understanding the Butterfly Effect."

anywhere from 75-90 percent of change efforts fail[717] and invariably the root cause indicates the leader was not prepared and/or did not prepare the organization for the uncertainty, stress, and anxiety that change precipitates within organizational members.[718] The organization needs you, the leader, to be the role model as change invariably occurs.[719] Take the initiative to begin your journey to the transformational level of leadership.

The Organization

The organization needs its members to contribute if it is to survive and it needs its members to be affectively committed if it is to prosper and to innovate. The difference between the two is leadership effectiveness.[720] Leadership effectiveness is the difference between positive organizational citizenship behaviors and the counterproductive work behaviors so often associated with low employee engagement scores.[721] This point is so obvious yet it is so often never considered[722] even as organizations retain global consultants and process improvement sensei to assist with workflow and innovation.[723]

The organization needs its leaders to understand the tension and the losses that result from a compliance and control or laissez-fair approach to leadership.[724] If

---

717 Anderson and Adams, *Mastering Leadership*.
718 Slattery, "Change Management."
719 Podsakoff et al., "Transformational Leader Behaviors and Follower Trust."
720 Anderson and Adams, *Mastering Leadership*.
721 Meisler et al., "Perceived Organizational Politics."
722 Anderson and Adams, *Mastering Leadership*.
723 Peter Block, *Flawless Consulting: A Guide to Getting Your Expertise Used* (San Francisco, CA: Jossey-Bass, 2011).
724 Anderson and Adams, *Mastering Leadership*.

you recall yet again your basic physical science classes you likely remember learning about magnets. Magnets attract or repulse depending upon their position. Distance of the magnet from the other magnet determines the degree or strength of the attraction or repulsion. Similarly, leaders attract or repel people depending upon their distance, i.e., their level of engagement. The concern is much deeper, the issue more nuanced however if you accept that controlling behaviors repulse relationships while a compliance orientation repels achievement.[725] These concepts have inverse relationships just as the opposite poles of magnets do…try as you will the inverse relationships cannot be overcome. This becomes a systems dynamics concern within organizations given the tendency for individual leadership styles to abound.[726] Again, the difference, the vital system leverage point,[727] is leadership effectiveness and the outcome is either positive organizational citizenship behaviors or counterproductive work behaviors.[728] If your behavior as a leader is oriented to control and compliance or tends towards a laissez-fair approach[729] simply be aware that you are a direct contributor to the organization internally bleeding money to the detriment of all.

A key theme of this book is that leaders should be cognizant of and well versed in both people and process issues. Figure 27 depicts how the leader should

---

[725] Ibid.
[726] Virginia Richardson, "LDLS741: Systems Dynamic Workshop," Regent Blackboard, 2020.
[727] Meadows, *Leverage Points*.
[728] Meisler et al., "Perceived Organizational Politics."
[729] Anderson and Adams, *Mastering Leadership*.

be oriented towards converting those engaged in counterproductive work behaviors to being positive contributors to organizational citizenship behaviors.[730] Think dollar signs when you ponder Figure 27 because such an approach directly stops the aforementioned bleeding of money. Part of the author's work includes showing how this can be monetized. It has been eye opening to many.

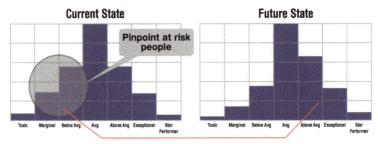

Figure 27: Recovering the Disengaged Employees

COURAGE

The Charge of the Light Brigade[731] poem, Figure 28, represents the finest in personal courage; however, in the workplace failing to reply or to reason is not the mark of courage.[732] This approach, sometimes referred to in the workplace as "just shut up and color", does not bode well for transformative efforts. Do not be blind to the perils of

---

730   Meisler et al., "Perceived Organizational Politics."
731   Alfred Tennyson, "The Charge of the Light Brigade," Poetry Foundation, 2017, https://www.poetryfoundation.org/poems/45319/the-charge-of-the-light-brigade.
732   Santisi et al., "The Role of Courage."

change even as you face the fact change is perilous for the leader responsible: There simply is no safe way to lead change[733] because, once started, it may take a form that was not anticipated if the design effort was not well planned, and even with excellent foresight and design, change may still cascade out of control.[734]

"...Theirs not to make reply, Theirs not to reason why, Theirs but to do and die: Into the valley of Death Rode the six hundred..."

Figure 28: Charge of the Light Brigade

It is within this environment that the leader's mettle is tested to the extreme given the pressure to perform, internal politics, and the allure of bonuses and greater compensation. Be true to yourself, i.e., do not allow your personal integrity to be compromised. It is within this environment that your personal values and beliefs will be challenged. Do not go along to get along; however, do not be an impediment just to make a point. If you are not self-employed then your compensation originates from an organization that is paying you to perform. You accepted the compensation and the terms. Align, be

---
733 Anderson and Adams, *Mastering Leadership*.
734 Hershman, "Harnessing the Power of Process."

loyal, and perform at the highest level. Lead by example. Or move on. Culture matters. If you are not a good fit you will know it. If the culture is not in a planned shift where you will fit then conform. Or move on. Hard words and intentionally so but courage to speak truth to power also requires self-awareness and respect for others. Too many in leadership positions simply breathe good air and offer no value, or worse, act as a detractor to others' success. These leaders impede transformation, cause harm to the organization, and preclude attainment of the leadership imperative. Do not be that guy.

It takes courage to be a leader. This courage takes many forms as you balance your needs with those of the organization and with the people you lead.

Enjoy.

SUMMARY

- Leader Engagement is the antidote to low Employee Engagement.
- Vision Casting and Communication are two vital leader competencies. Master both.
- You must undergo a metamorphosis to become a transformational leader. Start today.
- Courage takes many forms. Be brave in your leadership journey.
- Enjoy. Challenges are ever present but being in leadership is an honor as well as a burden. Go forth and do great things.

Bibliography

Adams, Scott. "Goals vs. Systems." Scott Adams' Blog, 2013. https://www.scottadamssays.com/2013/11/18/goals-vs-systems/.

Ahmad, Abad. "Management by Human Values: An Overview." *Journal of Human Values* 5, no. 1 (1999): 15–23. https://doi.org/10.1177/097168589900500103.

Alnajem, Mohamad. "Learning by Doing: An Undergraduate Lean A3 Project in a Kuwaiti Bank." *The TQM Journal* 33, no. 1 (2020): 71-94. https://doi.org/10.1108/tqm-01-2020-0010.

Amarantou, Vasiliki, Stergiani Kazakopoulou, Dimitrios Chatzoudes, and Prodromos Chatzoglou. "Resistance to Change: An Empirical Investigation of Its Antecedents." *Journal of Organizational Change Management* 31, no. 2 (2018): 426–50. https://doi.org/10.1108/jocm-05-2017-0196.

Anderson, Donald L. *Organizational development: The process of leading organizational change.* Los Angeles, CA: Sage, 2012.

Anderson, Robert J., and W. A. Adams. *Mastering Leadership: An Integrated Framework for Breakthrough Performance and Extraordinary Business Results.* Hoboken, NJ: Wiley. 2016.

Anderson, Virginia, and Lauren Johnson. *Systems Thinking Basics : From Concepts to Causal Loops.* Cambridge, MA: Pegasus Communications. 1997.

Antonakis, John, Neal M. Ashkanasy, and Marie T. Dasborough. "Does Leadership Need Emotional Intelligence?" *The Leadership Quarterly* 20, no. 2 (2009): 247–61. https://doi.org/10.1016/j.leaqua.2009.01.006.

Atwater, J. Bryan, and Satya S. Chakravorty. "Using the Theory of Constraints to Guide the Implementation of Quality Improvement Projects in Manufacturing Operations." *International Journal of Production Research* 33, no. 6 (1995): 1737–60. https://doi.org/10.1080/00207549508930240.

Baldoni, John. *Great Communication Secrets of Great Leaders*. New York, NY: Mcgraw-Hill Education – Europe, 2003.

Bartlett, Randy. *A Practitioner's Guide to Business Analytics: Using Data Analysis Tools to Improve Your Organization's Decision Making and Strategy.* New York: Mcgraw-Hill, 2013.

Bell, Alexander Graham. "Alexander Graham Bell Quotes." BrainyQuote.com, 2021. Alexander Graham Bell - Concentrate all your thoughts upon... (brainyquote.com).

Berenschot Quote from Ten Have, Steven, John Rijsman, Wouter Ten Have, and Joris Westhof. *The Social Psychology of Change Management Theories and an Evidence-Based Perspective on Social and Organizational Beings.* Routledge, 2018.

Berkun, Scott. *The Myths of Innovation* (Sebastopol, CA: O'Reilly Media, 2007).

Bhasin, Hitesh. "Importance of Environmental Scanning." Marketing91, 2019. https://www.marketing91.com/environmental-scanning.

Bhattacharyya, A. "Conventional Management Approach Is a Misfit Today, Says Vector Consulting Director. Business Today, 2016. https://www.businesstoday.in/opinion/interviews/conventional-management-approach-is-a-misfit-today-vector-consulting-director/story/235950.html.

Block, Peter. *Flawless Consulting: A Guide to Getting Your Expertise Used.* San Francisco, CA: Jossey-Bass, 2011.

Bonaparte, Napolean. "The Amateurs Discuss Tactics: The Professionals Discuss Logistics." Quotefancy.com, (n.d.). https://quotefancy.com/quote/870186/Napoleon-The-amateurs-discuss-tactics-the-professionals-discuss-logistics.

Bonaparte, Napolean. "A Soldier Will Fight Long and Hard for a Bit of Colored Ribbon." BrainyQuote.com, (n.d.). https://www.brainyquote.com/quotes/napoleon_bonaparte_108401.

Bronzo, Marcelo, Paulo Tarso Vilela de Resende, Marcos Paulo Valadares de Oliveira, Kevin P. McCormack, Paulo Renato de Sousa, and Reinaldo Lopes Ferreira. "Improving Performance Aligning Business Analytics with Process Orientation." *International Journal of Information Management* 33, no. 2 (2013): 300–307. https://doi.org/10.1016/j.ijinfomgt.2012.11.011.

Brubaker, David, Cinnie Noble, Richard Fincher, Susan Kee-Young Park, and Sharon Press. "Conflict Resolution in the Workplace: What Will the Future Bring?" *Conflict Resolution Quarterly* 31, no. 4 (2014): 357–86. https://doi.org/10.1002/crq.21104.

Buckingham, Marcus, and Donald O. Clifton. *Now, Discover Your Strengths: How to Develop Your Talents and Those of the People You Manage.* London: Pocket Books, 2005.

Burke, Warner, W. *Organization Change Theory and Practice.* Los Angeles, CA: Sage, 2018.

Caldecott, Tom. "World War II Program Helps Manufacturers Stay Lean." AllBusiness.com, 2010. https://www.allbusiness.com/world-war-ii-program-helps-manufacturers-stay-lean-11648305-1.html.

Caligiuri, Paula. *Cultural Agility: Building a Pipeline of Successful Global Professionals.* San Francisco, CA: Jossey-Bass, 2012.

Cameron, Kim, and Robert Quinn. *Diagnosing and Changing Organizational Culture: Based on the Competing Values Framework.* San Francisco, CA: Jossey-Bass, 2011.

Canton, James. *Future Smart: Managing the Game-Changing Trends That Will Transform Your World.* Boston, MA: Da Capo Press, A Member Of The Perseus Books Group, 2016.

Carnegie, Dale. "Inspiring Quotes by Dale Carnegie." Optimize, 2021. "Remember that a person's name is to that person the sweetest sound and most important sound in any language." | Optimize.

Carter, Tony. "Global Leadership." *Journal of Management Policy and Practice* 14, no. 1 (2013): 69-74.

CDC. "The Value of Systems Thinking." YouTube, 2017. https://www.youtube.com/watch?v=Fo3ndxVOZEo&feature=youtu.be.

Center, Deborah L. "Three as of Civility: Acknowledgment, Authentic Conversations, and Action." Edited by Diane M. Billings and Karren Kowalski. *The Journal of Continuing Education in Nursing* 41, no. 11 (2010): 488–89. https://doi.org/10.3928/00220124-20101026-04.

Chakravorty, Satya S., and J. Bryan Atwater. "How Theory of Constraints can be used to direct Preventive Maintenance." *Industrial Management* 36, no. 6 (1994): 10. http://eres.regent.edu:2048/login?url=https://search-proquest-com.ezproxy.regent.edu/docview/211615719?accountid=13479.

Chatterjee, Debashis. "Wise Ways." *Journal of Human Values* 12, no. 2 (2006): 153–60. https://doi.org/10.1177/097168580601200204.

Chermack, Thomas J. *Scenario Planning in Organizations: How to Create, Use, and Assess Scenarios.* San Francisco, CA: Berrett-Koehler, 2011.

Church, Allan H. "The Art and Science of Evaluating Organization Development Interventions." *OD Practitioner* 49, no. 2 (2017): 26-35.

Cialdini, Robert B. *Influence: Science and Practice.* Boston, MA: Pearson Education, 2009.

Ciulla, Joanne B. *Ethics: The Heart of Leadership.* Santa Barbara, CA: Praeger, 2014.

Colan, Lee. "12 Quotes to help You build more Powerful Relationships." Inc.com, March 30, 2016. 12 Quotes to Help You Build More Powerful Relationships | Inc.com.

Collyer, Mark. "Communication - the Route to Successful Change Management: Lessons from the Guinness Integrated Business Programme." *Measuring Business*

Excellence 5, no. 2 (2001). https://doi.org/10.1108/mbe.2001.26705bab.002.

Congressional Research Service. "Defense Primer: Department of Defense Maintenance Depots." Congressional Research Service. November 7, 2017. Defense Primer: Department of Defense Maintenance Depots (fas.org).

Crist, Eileen. "Reimagining the Human." *Science* 362, no. 6420 (2018): 1242–44. https://doi.org/10.1126/science.aau6026.

Cuddy, Amy. "Your Body Language May Shape Who You Are | Amy Cuddy." YouTube, 2012. https://www.youtube.com/watch?v=Ks-_Mh1QhMc.

Daniels, Aubrey C. *Performance Management: Changing Behavior That Drives Organizational Effectiveness.* Atlanta, GA: Performance Management Publications, 2014.

Dappa, Kelsey, Feyza Bhatti, and Ahmad Aljarah. "A Study on the Effect of Transformational Leadership on Job Satisfaction: The Role of Gender, Perceived Organizational Politics and Perceived Organizational Commitment." *Management Science Letters* (2019): 823–34. https://doi.org/10.5267/j.msl.2019.3.006.

Davis, Crystal J. *Servant Leadership and Followership: Examining the Impact on Workplace Behavior.* Cham, Switzerland: Palgrave Macmillan, 2017.

DellaVecchio, Dorena, and Bruce E. Winston. "A Seven-Scale Instrument to Measure the Romans 12 Motivational Gifts and a Proposition that the Romans 12 Gift Profiles might apply to Person-Job Fit Analysis." Published by the School of Leadership Studies, Regent University. 2004.

Denning, Stephen. *The Secret Language of Leadership: How Leaders Inspire Action through Narrative.* San Francisco, CA: Jossey-Bass, J. Wiley, 2007.

Diamandis, Peter H., and Steven Kotler. *The Future Is Faster than You Think: How Converging Technologies Are Transforming Business, Industries, and Our Lives.* New York, NY: Simon & Schuster Paperbacks, 2020.

Diamandis, Peter H., and Steven Kotler. *Bold: How to Go Big, Create Wealth and Impact the World.* London: Simon & Schuster, 2015.

Drew, Glenys M. 2010. "Enabling or 'Real' Power and Influence in Leadership." *Journal of Leadership Studies* 4, no. 1 (2010): 47–58. https://doi.org/10.1002/jls.20154.

Duan, Yanqing, Guangming Cao, and John S. Edwards. "Understanding the Impact of Business Analytics on Innovation." *European Journal of Operational Research,* (June 2018). https://doi.org/10.1016/j.ejor.2018.06.021.

Duignan, Brian. "Occam's Razor | Origin, Examples, & Facts." In *Encyclopædia Britannica,* (2018). https://www.britannica.com/topic/Occams-razor.

Dukes, Elizabeth. "The Employee Experience: What It Is and Why It Matters." Inc.com, August 31, 2017. https://www.inc.com/elizabeth-dukes/the-employee-experience-what-it-is-and-why-it-matt.html.

Düren, Petra. "Change Communication Can Be So Simple! The Empathic Change Communication Style." *Library Management* 37, no. 8/9 (2016): 398–409. https://doi.org/10.1108/lm-01-2016-0006.

Eby, Kate. "Everything You Need to Know about Theory of Constraints | Smartsheet." Smartsheet.com. July 24, 2017. https://www.smartsheet.com/all-about-theory-of-constraints.

Eby, Kate. "Everything You Need to Know about Lean Six Sigma | Smartsheet." Smartsheet.com. June 16, 2017. https://www.smartsheet.com/all-about-lean-six-sigma.

Eby, Kate. "Getting Started with Work Breakdown Structures (WBS) | Smartsheet." Smartsheet.com. November 8, 2016. https://www.smartsheet.com/getting-started-work-breakdown-structures-wbs.

Eby, Kate. "Everything You Need to Know about Agile Project Management | Smartsheet." Smartsheet.com. September 23, 2016. https://www.smartsheet.com/everything-you-need-to-know-about-agile-project-management.

Evergreen, Stephanie. "Presenting Data Effectively." Archived Webinar, 2017. SAGE Publishing.

Fisher, Roger, William Ury, and Bruce Patton. *Getting to Yes: Negotiating Agreement Without Giving In.* New York, NY: Houghton Mifflin, 1991.

Fitzpatrick, Sarah. "Why the Strategic National Stockpile isn't meant to solve a Crisis like Coronavirus." nbcnews.com. March 28, 2020. Why the Strategic National Stockpile isn't meant to solve a crisis like coronavirus (nbcnews.com).

George, Michael L., David Rowlands, Marc Price, and John Maxey. *The Lean Six Sigma Pocket Toolbook: A Quick Reference Guide to Nearly 100 Tools for Improving Process Quality, Speed, and Complexity.* New York: Toronto: Mcgraw-Hill, 2005.

Ghorbani, Shohreh. "The Philosophy behind S-Curves." YouTube, 2017. https://www.youtube.com/watch?v=2s6SEYvRd-vc&list=PLI-qstduR-XY47y2x4CUZDeh0uiodqPJn.

Gilbert, Dan. "The Psychology of Your Future Self." YouTube, 2014. https://www.youtube.com/watch?v=XNbaR54Gpj4.

Gilbert, Jacqueline A., Deana M. Raffo, and Toto Sutarso. "Gender, Conflict, and Workplace Bullying: Is Civility Policy the Silver Bullet?" *Journal of Managerial* Issues 25, no. 1 (2013): 79-98. Accessed June 22, 2021. http://www.jstor.org/stable/43488159.

Gimenez-Espin, Juan Antonio, Daniel Jiménez-Jiménez, and Micaela Martínez-Costa. "Organizational Culture for Total Quality Management." *Total Quality Management & Business Excellence* 24, no. 5-6 (2013): 678–92. https://doi.org/10.1080/14783363.2012.707409.

Goldstein, Daniel. "The Battle between Your Present and Future Self." YouTube, 2011. https://www.youtube.com/watch?v=t1Z_oufuQg4.

Graen, George B., and Mary Uhl-Bien. "Relationship-Based Approach to Leadership: Development of Leader-Member Exchange (LMX) Theory of Leadership over 25 Years: Applying a Multi-Level Multi-Domain Perspective." *The*

Leadership Quarterly 6, no. 2 (1995): 219–47. https://doi.org/10.1016/1048-9843(95)90036-5.

Greybey, James. "NatGeo's 'Year Million' is an Educational 'Black Mirror.'" Inverse, 2017. Accessed June 22, 2021. https://www.inverse.com/article/31604-year-million-national-geographic-documentary-black-mirror-ai-future.

Gunkel, Marjaana, Christopher Schlägel, and Robert L. Engle. "Culture's Influence on Emotional Intelligence: An Empirical Study of Nine Countries." *Journal of International Management* 20, no. 2 (2014): 256–74. https://doi.org/10.1016/j.intman.2013.10.002.

Guo, Yongxing, Haiying Kang, Bo Shao, and Beni Halvorsen. "Organizational Politics as a Blindfold." *Personnel Review* 48, no. 3 (2019): 784–98. https://doi.org/10.1108/pr-07-2017-0205.

Hammel, Gary. *Leading the Revolution: How to Thrive in Turbulent Times by making Innovation a Way of Life.* Boston, MA: Penguin Books, Ltd, 2002.

Handbook 15-06. *MDMP: Lessons and best practices.* US Army Combined Arms Center, 2015. https://usacac.army.mil/sites/default/files/publications/15-06_0.pdf.

Hao, Q., Shi, Y., and Yang, W. "How Leader-Member Exchange Affects Knowledge Sharing Behavior: Understanding the Effects of Commitment and Employee Characteristics." *Frontiers in Psychology* 10, (2019). https://doi.org/10.3389/fpsyg.2019.02768.

Hershman, Lisa. "Harnessing the Power of Process." Hammer and Company Seminar Lecture, 2010.

Hessing, Ted. "Pareto Analysis." 6σstudyguide.com, (n.d). https://sixsigmastudyguide.com/pareto-analysis/.

Hille, Peter, and Christoph Hasselbach. "Capitol Hill Riots: Are Western Democracies under Attack?" dw.com, 2021. https://www.msn.com/en-us/news/world/capitol-hill-riots-are-western-democracies-under-attack/ar-BB1cyzLU.

Hills, Russell. "Statistical Process Control Basic Control Charts." YouTube, 2015. https://www.youtube.com/watch?v=WdqSm0DiYtY.

Hofstede, Geert, Gert Jan Hofstede, and Michael Minkov. *Cultures and Organizations: Software of the Mind: Intercultural Cooperation and Its Importance for Survival.* Johanneshov: Mtm, 2017.

Invernizzi, Emanuele, Stefania Romenti, and Michela Fumagalli. "Identity, Communication and Change Management in Ferrari." Edited by John M.T. Balmer. *Corporate Communications: An International Journal* 17, no. 4 (2012): 483–97. https://doi.org/10.1108/13563281211274194.

Jacob, Dee, Suzan Bergland, and Jeff Cox. *Velocity: Combining Lean, Six Sigma, and the Theory of Constraints to Achieve Breakthrough Performance.* New York, NY: Free Press, 2010.

Johansen, Bob. *New Leadership Literacies: Thriving in a Future of Extreme Disruption and Distributed Everything.* Berrett-Koehler Publishers, Inc, 2017.

Kanbanize. "Gemba Walk: Where the Real Work Happens." Kanban Software for Agile Project Management, n.d. https://kanbanize.com/lean-management/improvement/gemba-walk.

Kargas, Antonios D., and Dimitrios Varoutas. "On the Relation between Organizational Culture and Leadership: An Empirical Analysis." Edited by Tahir Nisar. *Cogent Business & Management* 2, no. 1 (2015). https://doi.org/10.1080/23311975.2015.1055953.

Katz, Neil H., and Linda T. Flynn. "Understanding Conflict Management Systems and Strategies in the Workplace: A Pilot Study." *Conflict Resolution Quarterly* 30, no. 4 (2013): 393–410. https://doi.org/10.1002/crq.21070.

Kauffman, Draper L. *Systems One: An Introduction to Systems Thinking.* The Future Systems Series, 1980.

Kelley, Katherine M., and Ryan S. Bisel. "Leaders' Narrative Sensemaking during LMX Role Negotiations: Explaining How Leaders Make Sense of Who to Trust and When." *The Leadership Quarterly* 25, no. 3 (2014): 433–48. https://doi.org/10.1016/j.leaqua.2013.10.011.

Kessler, Eric H. *Encyclopedia of management theory.* Los Angeles, CA: Sage Publications, 2003.

Kettering Global. "5 Steps to Understanding and Applying the Theory of Constraints." Kettering Global, July 25, 2016. https://online.kettering.edu/news/2016/07/25/5/-steps-understanding-and-applying-theory-of-constraints.

Kilkelly, Eddie. "Creating Leaders for Successful Change Management." *Strategic HR Review* 13, no. 3 (2014): 127–129. https://doi.org/10.1108/shr-01-2014-0004.

Kim, David, Dan Fisher, and David McCalman. "Modernism, Christianity, and Business Ethics: A Worldview Perspective." *Journal of Business Ethics* 90, no. 1 (2009): 115–21. https://doi.org/10.1007/s10551-009-0031-2.

Kinni, Theodore. "Seeing, Doing, and Imagining." Strategy+Business. Accessed June 22, 2021. https://www.strategy-business.com/blog/Seeing-doing-and-imagining?.

Kitchen, Philip J., and Finbarr Daly. "Internal Communication during Change Management." *Corporate Communications: An International Journal* 7, no. 1 (2002): 46–53. https://doi.org/10.1108/13563280210416035.

Kopf, Simon Maria. "A Problem for Dialogue: Can World-Views Be Rational?" *New Blackfriars* 100, no. 1087 (2017): 284–98. https://doi.org/10.1111/nbfr.12328.

Kouzes, James M., & Barry Z Posner. *The Leadership Challenge: How to Make Extraordinary Things Happen in Organizations.* San Francisco, CA: Jossey-Bass, 2012.

Kruse, Kevin. "100 Best Quotes on Leadership." Forbes. Accessed June 22, 2021. https://www.forbes.com/sites/kevinkruse/2012/10/16/quotes-on-leadership/?sh=38a9f3102feb.

Lake, Alan. "Tipping Point for Islamic Domination = 20% of Population." 4freedoms.com, 2015. http://4freedoms.com/video/how-islam-is-taking-over-the-world-islamization-explained.

Landau, Peter. "A Quick Guide to Float (or Slack) in Project Management." ProjectManager.com, June 24, 2020. https://

www.projectmanager.com/blog/float-in-project-management.

Lawler, Alan. "LMS Transitioning to Moodle: A Surprising Case of Successful, Emergent Change Management." *Australasian Journal of Educational Technology* 27, no. 7 (2011). https://doi.org/10.14742/ajet.907.

Lawrence, Jamie. 2016. "What Are the Causes & Nature of Employee Disengagement?" HRZone, July 18, 2016. https://www.hrzone.com/engage/employees/what-are-the-causes-nature-of-employee-disengagement.

Lawrence, Paul. "Leading Change – Insights into How Leaders Actually Approach the Challenge of Complexity." *Journal of Change Management* 15, no. 3 (2015): 231–52. https://doi.org/10.1080/14697017.2015.1021271.

Le Blanc, Pascale M., and Vicente González-Romá. "A Team Level Investigation of the Relationship between Leader–Member Exchange (LMX) Differentiation, and Commitment and Performance." *The Leadership Quarterly* 23, no. 3 (2012): 534–44. https://doi.org/10.1016/j.leaqua.2011.12.006.

Lee, HeeKap. "Jesus Teaching Through Discovery." *International Christian Community of Teacher Educators Journal* 1, no. 2 (2006).

Lepera, Nicole. 2019. "How to Future-Self-Journal." YouTube, 2019. https://www.youtube.com/watch?v=vhaX1CeQGCk.

Levin, M. "The Top 10 Leadership Blind Spots, and 5 Ways to Turn Them into Strengths." Inc.com, July 13, 2017. The Top 10 Leadership Blind Spots, and 5 Ways to Turn Them Into Strengths | Inc.com.

Li, Xin, Qianqian Xie, Jiaojiao Jiang, Yuan Zhou, and Lucheng Huang. "Identifying and Monitoring the Development Trends of Emerging Technologies Using Patent Analysis and Twitter Data Mining: The Case of Perovskite Solar Cell Technology." *Technological Forecasting and Social Change* 146 (September 2019): 687–705. https://doi.org/10.1016/j.techfore.2018.06.004.

Lipman, Victor. 2016. "Why Does Organizational Change Usually Fail? New Study Provides Simple Answer."

Forbes, 2016. https://www.forbes.com/sites/victorlipman/2016/02/08/why-does-organizational-change-usually-fail-new-study-provides-simple-answer/#658440674bf8.

"Little's Law - Overview, Formula and Practical Example." Corporate Finance Institute, 2019. https://corporatefinanceinstitute.com/resources/knowledge/other/littles-law/.

Littlefield, Matthew L. "Manufacturing Metrics: First Pass Yield Benchmark Data." January 24, 2013. Manufacturing Metrics: First Pass Yield Benchmark Data (lnsresearch.com).

Lot, Luciana Teixeira, Alice Sarantopoulos, Li Li Min, Simone Reges Perales, Ilka de Fatima Santana Ferreira Boin, and Elaine Cristina de Ataide. "Using Lean Tools to Reduce Patient Waiting Time." *Leadership in Health Services* 31, no. 3 (2018): 343–51. https://doi.org/10.1108/lhs-03-2018-0016.

Mahmoudi, Amin, and Mohammad Reza Feylizadeh. "A Grey Mathematical Model for Crashing of Projects by Considering Time, Cost, Quality, Risk and Law of Diminishing Returns." *Grey Systems: Theory and Application* 8, no. 3 (2018): 272–94. https://doi.org/10.1108/gs-12-2017-0042.

Manson, Steven M. "Simplifying Complexity: A Review of Complexity Theory." *Geoforum* 32, no. 3 (2001): 405–14. https://doi.org/10.1016/s0016-7185(00)00035-x.

Martin, Jeffery. "Trump Signs Emergency Bill to Make Companies Manufacture Medical Supplies to Fight Coronavirus." Newsweek. March 18, 2020. Trump Signs Emergency Bill to Make Companies Manufacture Medical Supplies to Fight Coronavirus (newsweek.com).

Mathew, Molly and Gupta, K. S. "Transformational Leadership: Emotional Intelligence." *SCMS Journal of Indian Management* 12, no. 2 (2015): 75-89.

McAteer, Teal. "Top 3 Tips for Understanding How Thinking Affects Behaviour." n.d. DeGroote School of Business, 2016. https://www.degroote.mcmaster.ca/articles/top-3-tips-understanding-thinking-affects-behaviour/.

McKinsey and Company. "Enduring Ideas: The 7-S Framework." McKinsey Quarterly, 2008, March 1. Enduring Ideas: The 7-S Framework | McKinsey.

Meadows, Donella H. *Leverage Points: Places to Intervene in a System.* Hartland Four Corners, VT: Sustainability Institute, 1999.

Meadows, Donella H. *Dancing with Systems: An Excerpt from her Unfinished Manuscript Thinking in Systems.* Whole Earth Review, 2001.

Mehall, Scott. "Purposeful Interpersonal Interaction and the Point of Diminishing Returns for Graduate Learners." *The Internet and Higher Education* 48, (January 2021): 100774. https://doi.org/10.1016/j.iheduc.2020.100774.

Meisler, Galit, Amos Drory, and Eran Vigoda-Gadot. "Perceived Organizational Politics and Counterproductive Work Behavior." *Personnel Review ahead-of-print,* (2019). https://doi.org/10.1108/pr-12-2017-0392.

Michalko, Michael. *Thinkertoys: A Handbook of Creative-Thinking Techniques.* Berkeley, CA: Ten Speed Press, 2006.

Modi, Kartik, Harshal Lowalekar, and N.M.K. Bhatta. "Revolutionizing Supply Chain Management the Theory of Constraints Way: A Case Study." *International Journal of Production Research* 57, no. 11 (2018): 3335–61. https://doi.org/10.1080/00207543.2018.1523579.

Morgan, Gareth. *Images of Organizations.* Thousand Oaks, CA: Sage Publications, Inc, 2006.

Moslemi, Amelia. "Essential Attributes and Behaviours of a Change Leader." Queens University IRC, 2011.

Motzko, S. M. "Deming's 14 Points for Management: Variation, System Improvement." *Professional Safety,* 34, no. 8 (1989).

Mulholland, Ben. "Little's Law: How to Analyze Your Processes (with Stealth Bombers)." Process Street, November 20, 2017. https://www.process.st/littles-law/.

Mike Murdock. "The secret of your future is hidden in your daily routine." BrainyQuote.com, 2021. Future Quotes - BrainyQuote.

Murrar, Sohad, and Markus Brauer. "Overcoming Resistance to Change: Using Narratives to Create More Positive Intergroup Attitudes." *Current Directions in Psychological*

Science, (February 2019). 096372141881855. https://doi.org/10.1177/0963721418818552.

Napier, Nancy K. "The Myth of Multitasking: Think You can Multitask Well? Think Again." *Psychology Today,* (May 12, 2014). The Myth of Multitasking | Psychology Today.

Nelissen, Paul, and Martine van Selm. "Surviving Organizational Change: How Management Communication Helps Balance Mixed Feelings." *Corporate Communications: An International Journal* 13, no. 3 (2008): 306–18. https://doi.org/10.1108/13563280810893670.

New American Standard Bible. Lockman Foundation,1995. https://bible.knowing-jesus.com.

Newman, A., G. Schwarz, B. Cooper, and S. Sendjaya. "How Servant Leadership Influences Organizational Citizenship Behavior: The Roles of LMX, Empowerment, and Proactive Personality." *Journal of Business Ethics* 145, no. 1 (2015): 49–62. https://doi.org/10.1007/s10551-015-2827-6.

Nicasio, Francesca. "Inventory Turnover 101: What It Is and How to Get It Right." Vend Retail Blog, May 11, 2020. https://www.vendhq.com/blog/inventory-turnover/.

Northouse, Peter Guy. *Leadership: Theory and Practice.* Thousand Oaks, CA: Sage Publishing, 2016.

Oster, Gary. "Listening to Luddites: Innovation Antibodies and Corporate Success." Regent Blackboard, (n.d).

Oxford Reference. "Helmuth von Moltke 1800-91 Prussian Military Commander." Oxford Press, 2021. Helmuth von Moltke - Oxford Reference.

Parker, Christina. "Practicing Conflict Resolution and Cultural Responsiveness within Interdisciplinary Contexts: A Study of Community Service Practitioners." *Conflict Resolution Quarterly* 32, no. 3 (2015): 325–57. https://doi.org/10.1002/crq.21115.

Patton, George S. "Watch What People Are Cynical About, and You Can Discover What They Lack." BrainyQuote.com, (n.d). www.brainyquote.com/authors/george-s-patton-quotes.

Patton, George S. "Don't Tell People How to do Things, Tell Them What to do and Let Them Surprise You with the Results." BrainyQuote.com, (n.d.). https://www.brainyquote.com/quotes/george_s_patton_159766.

Pickford, Helen Campbell, and Genevieve Joy. "Organisational Citizenship Behaviours: Definitions and Dimensions." *SSRN Electronic Journal,* (2016). https://doi.org/10.2139/ssrn.2893021.

Podsakoff, Philip M., Scott B. MacKenzie, Robert H. Moorman, and Richard Fetter. "Transformational Leader Behaviors and Their Effects on Followers' Trust in Leader, Satisfaction, and Organizational Citizenship Behaviors." *The Leadership Quarterly* 1, no. 2 (1990): 107–42. https://doi.org/10.1016/1048-9843(90)90009-7.

Porath, Christine Lynne. *Mastering Civility: A Manifesto for the Workplace.* New York, NY: Grand Central Publishing, 2016.

Reinhard, Beth, and Emma Brown. "Face Masks and National Stockpile have not been substantially replenished since 2009." The Washington Post. March 10, 2020. Face masks in national stockpile of medical supplies have not been substantially replenished since 2009 - The Washington Post.

Richardson, Virginia. "LDLS741: Systems Dynamic Workshop." Regent Blackboard, 2020.

Robbins, Vernon K. *Exploring the Texture of Texts: A Guide to Socio-Rhetorical Interpretation.* New York, NY: Bloomsbury Publishing Plc, 2012.

Robertson, Donald J. "The Stoicism of Benjamin Franklin." Medium, February 5, 2020. https://medium.com/stoicism-philosophy-as-a-way-of-life/the-stoicism-of-benjamin-franklin-21ed64abb4ab.

Rokeach, Milton. *The Nature of Human Values.* New York, NY: Free Press, 1973.

Sagan, Carl. "Knowing a Great Deal…" Goodreads.com, Accessed June 22, 2021. https://www.goodreads.com/quotes/897642-knowing-a-great-deal-is-not-the-same-as-being.

Santisi, Giuseppe, Ernesto Lodi, Paola Magnano, Rita Zarbo, and Andrea Zammitti. 2020. "Relationship between Psychological Capital and Quality of Life: The Role of Courage." *Sustainability* 12, no. 13 (2020): 5238. https://doi.org/10.3390/su12135238.

Sarantopoulos, Alice, Li Li Min, Simone Reges Perales, Ilka de Fatima Santana Ferreira Boin, and Elaine Cristina de Ataide. "Using Lean Tools to Reduce Patient Waiting Time." *Leadership in Health Services* 31, no. 3 (2018): 343–51. https://doi.org/10.1108/lhs-03-2018-0016.

Sawyer, Ralph D. *Sun Tzu: Art of War.* Boulder, CO: Westview Press, 1994.

Schein, Edgar H. *Organizational Culture and Leadership.* New Jersey: Wiley, 2016.

Schneider, William E. "Why Good Management Ideas Fail": Strategy & Leadership 28, no. 1 (2000): 24–29. https://doi.org/10.1108/10878570010336001.

Schriesheim, Chester A., Stephanie L. Castro, and Claudia C. Cogliser. "Leader-Member Exchange (LMX) Research: A Comprehensive Review of Theory, Measurement, and Data-Analytic Practices." *The Leadership Quarterly* 10, no. 1 (1999): 63–113. https://doi.org/10.1016/s1048-9843(99)80009-5.

Senge, Peter M. *The Fifth Discipline Fieldbook.* London: N. Brealey, 1994.

Sharma, Ruchika. "12 Voice of the Customer Methodologies to Generate a Goldmine of Customer Feedback." Hubspot.com, 2019. https://blog.hubspot.com/service/voice-of-the-customer-methodologies.

Shin, Ho Wook, Joseph C. Picken, and Gregory G. Dess. "Revisiting the Learning Organization: How to Create It." *Organizational Dynamics* 46 (2017): 46-56.

Shore, David A. *Launching and Leading Change Initiatives in Health Care Organizations: Managing Successful Projects.* San Francisco, CA: Jossey-Bass, 2014.

Shrimpton, Daisy, Deborah McGann, and Leigh M. Riby. "Daydream Believer: Rumination, Self-Reflection and the

Temporal Focus of Mind Wandering Content." *Europe's Journal of Psychology* 13, no. 4 (2017): 794–809. https://doi.org/10.5964/ejop.v13i4.1425.

Simoes, Paula Matos Marques, Fundacao Dom Cabral, Belo Horizonte, and Mark Esposito. "Improving Change Management: How Communication Nature Influences Resistance to Change." *Journal of Management Development* 33, no. 4 (2014): 324–41. https://doi.org/10.1108/jmd-05-2012-0058.

Sin, Hock-Peng, Jennifer D. Nahrgang, and Frederick P. Morgeson. "Understanding Why They Don't See Eye to Eye: An Examination of Leader–Member Exchange (LMX) Agreement." *Journal of Applied Psychology* 94, no. 4 (2009): 1048–57. https://doi.org/10.1037/a0014827.

Singleton, Rachel, Leslie A. Toombs, Sonia Taneja, Charlotte Larkin, and Mildred Golden Pryor. "Workplace Conflict: A Strategic Leadership Imperative." *International Journal of Business & Public Administration* 8, no. 1 (2011): 149-163.

Slattery, Jeff. "Change Management." *Journal of Strategic Leadership,* 4, no. 2 (2013): 1-5. https://www.regent.edu/acad/global/publications/jsl/vol4iss2/jslvol4iss2.pdf#page=59.

Smith, Pearl R. "Enhancing Your Emotional Intelligence: Manage Emotions to get the Results You Want!" 2013. PowerPoint presentation to Mercer University MSOL students, McDonough, GA in 2017.

Sobek, Durward K., and Art Smalley. *Understanding A3 Thinking: A Critical Component of Toyota's PDCA Management System.* Boca Raton: CRC Press, 2008.

Sosik, John J., and Dongil Jung. *Full Range Leadership Development Pathways for People, Profit, and Planet.* New York, NY: Routledge, 2018.

Sowell, Thomas. "Thomas Sowell>Quotes>Quotable Quotes." Goodreads.com, 2021. Quote by Thomas Sowell: "There are no solutions. There are only trade-offs." (goodreads.com).

Spear, David, and Daly, D. "Lean Leader." Simpler, 2010, September 28.

Stanleigh, Michael. "Effecting Successful Change Management Initiatives." *Industrial and Commercial Training* 40, no 1. (2008): 34–37. https://doi.org/10.1108/00197850810841620.

Stavros, Jacqueline, David Cooperrider, and D. Lynn Kelley. "Strategic Inquiry with Appreciative Intent: Inspiration to SOAR!" *AI Practitioner: International Journal of Appreciative Inquiry* (2003).

Steers, Richard M., Carlos Sanchez-Runde, and Luciara Nardon. "Leadership in a Global Context: New Directions in Research and Theory Development." *Journal of World Business* 47, no. 4 (2012): 479–82. https://doi.org/10.1016/j.jwb.2012.01.001.

Ten Have, Steven, John Rijsman, Wouter Ten Have, and Joris Westhof. *The Social Psychology of Change Management Theories and an Evidence-Based Perspective on Social and Organizational Beings.* Routledge, 2018.

Tennyson, Alfred. "The Charge of the Light Brigade." Poetry Foundation, 2017. https://www.poetryfoundation.org/poems/45319/the-charge-of-the-light-brigade.

Thompkins, Shelley. "Leaders Level of Emotional Intelligence and Its Influence on Employee Engagement: A Case Study." PhD diss. Cappella University, 2015.

TOC Institute. "TOC in India." Theory of Constraints Institute, 2020. https://www.tocinstitute.org/toc-in-india.html.

Trabucchi, Daniel, Laurent Muzellec, and Sébastien Ronteau. "Sharing Economy: Seeing through the Fog." Internet Research, April 2019. https://doi.org/10.1108/intr-03-2018-0113.

Tzu, Lao. "He who knows others is wise; he who knows himself is enlightened." Goodreads.com, 2021. Know Thyself Quotes (249 quotes) (goodreads.com).

Udayar, Shagini, Marina Fiori, and Elise Bausseron. "Emotional Intelligence and Performance in a Stressful Task: The Mediating Role of Self-Efficacy." *Personality and Individual Differences* 156 (April 2020): 109790.

United States. Department Of The Army. *Army Leadership: Competent, Confident, and Agile.* Washington, DC: HQ., Dept. Of The Army. 2006.

University of Tennessee. *AFSO21: Air Force Smart Ops for the 21st Century.* The University of Tennessee Center for Executive Education, 2009.

Van Tongeren, Daryl R., Don E. Davis, Joshua N. Hook, and Charlotte vanOyen Witvliet. "Humility." *Current Directions in Psychological Science* 28, no. 5 (October 2019): 463–68. https://doi.org/10.1177/0963721419850153.

Vermeulen, Yan. "Lights Out: Manufacturing in the Dark." Odgers Berndtson, 2018. https://www.odgersberndtson.com/en-us/insights/manufacturing-in-the-dark.

Vernon, Jamie. "Understanding the Butterfly Effect." *American Scientist* 105, no. 3 (2017): 130. https://doi.org/10.1511/2017.105.3.130.

Vidgen, Richard, Sarah Shaw, and David B. Grant. "Management Challenges in Creating Value from Business Analytics." *European Journal of Operational Research* 261, no. 2 (2017): 626–39. https://doi.org/10.1016/j.ejor.2017.02.023.

Villanova University. " What is Critical Chain Project Management?" 2021. https://www.villanovau.com/resources/project-management/critical-chain-project-management/.

Volini, Erica, Kraig Eaton, Jeff Schwartz, David Mallon, Yves Van Durme, Maren Hauptmann, Rob Scott, and Shannon Poynton. "Diving Deeper." Deloitte Insights, 2020. https://www.deloitte.com/us/en/insights/focus/human-capital-trends/2021/workforce-trends-2020.html?id=us:2ps:3bi:-consem21:eng:cons:010721:nonem:na:88zvv7hb:1209959.

Wang, Jie, Grand H. L. Cheng, Tingting Chen, and Kwok Leung. "Team Creativity/Innovation in Culturally Diverse Teams: A Meta-Analysis." *Journal of Organizational Behavior* 40, no. 6 (2019): 693–708. https://doi.org/10.1002/job.2362.

Wang, Zhining, Dandan Liu, and Shaohan Cai. "Self-Reflection and Employee Creativity." *Chinese Management Studies*

13, no. 4 (2019): 895–917. https://doi.org/10.1108/cms-09-2018-0683.

Wang, Zhining, Shaohan Cai, Mengli Liu, Dandan Liu, and Lijun Meng. "The Effects of Self-Reflection on Individual Intellectual Capital." *Journal of Intellectual Capital* 21, no. 6 (2020): 1107–24. https://doi.org/10.1108/jic-03-2019-0043.

Weiner, Bryan J. "A Theory of Organizational Readiness for Change." *Implementation Science* 4, no. 1 (2009). https://doi.org/10.1186/1748-5908-4-67.

Wellers, Dan, and Kai Goerlich. "The Human Factor in an AI Future." SAP Insights, July 21, 2020. https://insights.sap.com/the-human-factor-in-an-ai-future/.

Will, Matthias Georg, and Ingo Pies. "Sensemaking and Sensegiving." *Journal of Accounting & Organizational Change* 14, no. 3 (2018): 291–313. https://doi.org/10.1108/jaoc-11-2016-0075.

CPSIA information can be obtained
at www.ICGtesting.com
Printed in the USA
BVHW090558020222
627775BV00022B/1617